THE WOMEN'S

EDITION 2024

100 WOMEN LEADERS
OF NATIONS AND PEOPLES

Richard O'Brien

The Women's 100:
100 Women Leaders of Nations and Peoples.
2024 Edition

Any photos not credited are public fair use images, many from Wikipedia, Twitter, Creative Commons and other free image resources. Special Thank You to Remini Enhancements used for enhancing many of the public domain photos. Cover Design: Jitender Kumar. Graphic Illustrations of Interior Portaits: Adel Berakdar.
ISBN: 979-8-9889139-3-1

THE WOMEN'S 100:

100 WOMEN LEADERS OF NATIONS AND PEOPLES.

2024 EDITION

By Richard O'Brien

2024 Edition

Any photos not credited are public fair use images, many from Wikipedia, Twitter, Creative Commons and other free image resources. Cover Design: Jitender Kumar. Graphic Illustrations of Interior Portraits: Adel Berakdar.
ISBN: 979-8-9889139-3-1

For my children.

WOMEN LEADERS OF NATIONS AND PEOPLES
TABLE OF CONTENTS

CHAPTER 1: YOUNG WOMEN LEADERS OF PEOPLES

CHAPTER 2. WOMEN LEADERS OF THE U.N.

CHAPTER 3: WOMEN LEADERS OF NORTH AMERICA

CHAPTER 4: WOMEN LEADERS OF SOUTH AMERICA

CHAPTER 7: WOMEN LEADERS OF THE EU & EUROPE

7

CHAPTER 8. WOMEN LEADERS OF AUSTRALIA AND THE PACIFIC RIM

* * *

FORWARD

This book was a joy to research and write. I originally wrote it for my daughter but ended up being caught up in the interesting stories of these women leaders. Some are as young as Greta Thunburg who bravely sailed acoss an ocean in a catamaran to chastise the leaders of the world on global warming. Her constituency is a generation who are effected most and usually have no place at the table. Or the talented young poet Emi Mahmoud who traversed Sudan by foot to create a grassroots peace movement and was appointed Goodwill Ambassador of the UN High Commissioner for Refugees. There are the effective leaders like Jacinda Ahern of New Zealand who kept her people safe from Covid, or the former rebel Dilma Roussef of Brazil who's code name was 'Estela,' or Bidhya Bandhari of Nepal who actually convinced the Moaist guerillas of her land to integrate and put down their arms. You will meet Natasa Micic who helped overthrow Serbia's dictator from her car with 'Thelma and Louise,' painted on it, who scant three years later rose to be the 'accidental' leader her country. There is the biologist Ameenah Gurib Fakim who elevated Mauritius' medical research or Catherine Samba Panza who presided over a free election and a cessation of the civil war in CAR, installed a democratically elected leader then selflessly resigned.

The past name for this book was 'Women Presidents and Prime Ministers.' We have changed the name and the format. More than 150 women have served as President or Prime Minister and the number is growing.. We vetted those who served for only for a few weeks, or for an uneventful year, or who's nation's population was tiny. We kept the most impactful women who have recently led nations or peoples.. We hope you enjoy our selections and are inspired. Maybe you will become one, or raise one, yourself.

Richard O'Brien
October, 2023.

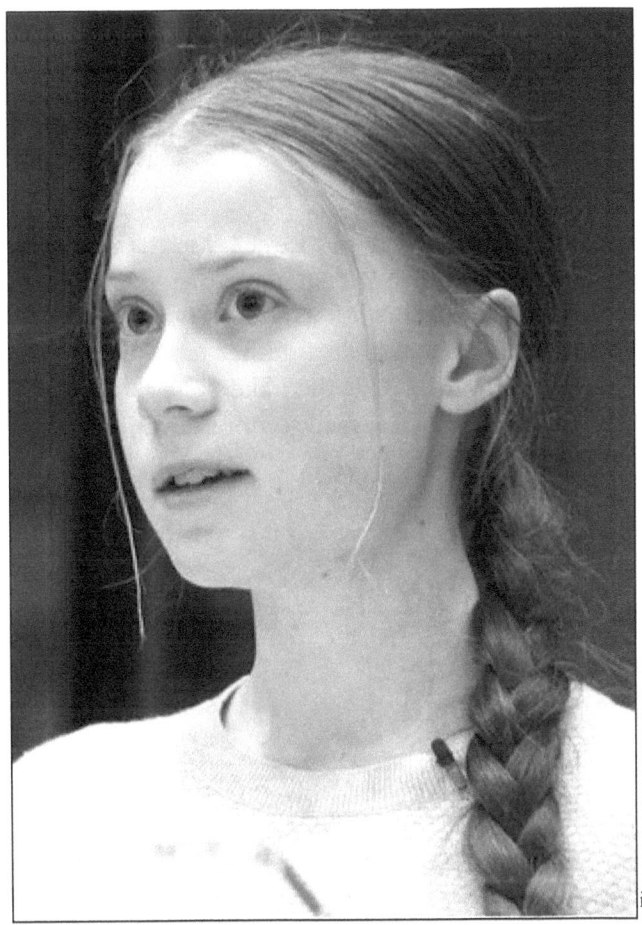

GRETA THUNBERG
Green Spokesperson/Representative for a Generation

Our profiles in leadership begins with youth. There is perhaps no better example of a single person who represents the hope, outrage and message of a generation than Greta Thurnberg.

Her story is the stuff of legends and mythology. She was the girl who crossed the sea in a sailboat to speak her angry truth to the most powerful leaders in the world. She brought a stern lecturing voice to upbraid the adults of the world on behalf of her generations and those to come to preserve the planet and reverse global warming that threatens to devastate the planet.

Greta was born in Stockholm, Sweden and was diagnosed as being on autism spectrum. She has said that while she takes things quite seriously, it allows her a singlemindedness of purpose which has had demonstratible results.

On August 20th, 2018, 15 year old Greta skipped school and began her protest outside of the Swedish Parliament. Unable to put the thoughts of global warming and its effect out of her head during school, her father relented and allowed her to dedicate herself to her protest. For several months it seemed like her protest was in vain, as policymakers and the public seemed to not see the girl often sitting in the rain with a faded placard.

She crossed the Atlantic Ocean in this craft.

At 15 years of she began protesting in front of the Swedish Parliament. She missed school and her parents consented to it because they knew the issue had become an all-consuming passion for her. In 2019, mindful of the carbon footprint of a single air flight, she boarded a rocking 60 foot catamarand sailboat and began her perilous journey across the Atlantic Ocean to speak truth to power Upon her arrival, she took her place on the first day of the --- conference and delivered what is arguably the most important speech of the modern age. Sje was featured as Time Magazine's Person of the Year in 2019, the youngest ever selected for that honor. Her words, found their mark. The attendees set the most ambitious climate change response agenda as a result.

"This is all wrong. I shouldn't be up here. I should be back in school on the other side of the ocean. Yet you all come to us young people for hope. How dare you?

You have stolen my dreams and my childhood with your empty words, and yet I'm one of the lucky ones. People are suffering, people are dying. Entire ecosystems are collapsing. We are in the beginning of a mass extinction and all you can talk about is money and fairytales of eternal economic growth. How dare you?

For more than 30 years, the science has been crystal clear. How dare you continue to look away and come here saying that you're doing enough when the politics and solutions needed are still nowhere in sight? You say you hear us and that you understand the urgency, but no matter how sad and angry I am, I do not want to believe that. Because if you really understood the situation and still kept on failing to act, then you would be evil and that I refuse to believe.

The popular idea of cutting our emissions in half in ten years only gives us a 50 percent chance of staying below 1.5 degrees and the risk of setting up irreversible chain reactions beyond human control. Fifty percent may be acceptable to you, but those numbers do not include tipping points most feedback loops, additional warming hidden by toxic air pollution, or the aspects of equity and climate justice.

They also rely on my generation sucking hundreds of billions of tons of your CO_2 out of the air with technologies that barely exist. So a 50 percent risk is simply not acceptable to us. We who have to live with the consequences. To have a 67 percent chance of staying below the 1.5 degree of temperature rise, the best odds given by the IPCC, the world had 420 gigatons of CO_2 left to emit back on January 1, 2018.

Today that figure is already down to less than 350 gigatons. How dare you pretend that this can be solved with just business as usual and some technical solutions? With today's emissions levels, that remaining CO2 that entire budget will be gone is less than 8 and a half years. There will not be any solutions or plans presented in line with these figures here today because these numbers are too uncomfortable and you are still not mature enough to tell it like it is.

You are failing us, but young people are starting to understand your betrayal. The eyes of all future generations are upon you. And if you choose to fail us, I say we will never forgive you. We will not let you get away with this, right here, right now, is where we draw the line. The world is waking up, and change is coming whether you like it or not."[1]

To this day, she continues to get arrested, speak out and speak truth to power, representing the view of hundreds of millions of children and young people who are disenfranchised from the decisions which are causing irreparable damage to our planet.

---

[1] https://www.pbs.org/newshour/world/read-climate-activist-greta-thunbergs-speech-to-the-un

iii

MALALA YOUSAFZAI
Spokesperson/Rep. 130 Million Repressed Girls

The daughter of a teacher in a rural town in Pakistan, when the Taliban (know for their power in Afghanistan) took over her town and girls were no longer allowed in school. Malala began writing a blog at the age of 11 under the pseudonym 'Gul Makai' describing conditions under Taliban rule. Walking home one day a gunman asked if she was Malala and shot her in the head. Ten days later she emerged from a coma and had to make a decision. She was given the miracle of surviving an assassination attempt, should she live a quiet life or redouble her effort to decry the injustices of the Taliban?[2] She chose the latter.

In the subsequent years, she has founded The Malala Fund which addresses and takes practical steps to remedy the 130 million girls who do not attend, are not allowed to attend school. In 2014 she won the Nobel Prize for literature and became the youngest recipient of that prestigious award. In 2020, she graduated form Oxford University and continues to run the Malala fund, working hard as ever to bring attention, funding and relief to her constituency of 130 million.[3]

[2] https://malala.org/malalas-story
[3] https://malala.org/malalas-story

Original Graphic Illustration of Emi Mahmoud by Adel Berakdar for Jenoco Publishing.

EMTITHAL (EMI) MAHMOUD
UNHCR
(United Nations High Commissioner for Refugees)
Goodwill Ambassador

There are currently more than 108 million forcibly people displaced by war and 35 million refugees. These people have two voices, the UN High Commissioner for Refugees, and a young woman. She is Emi Mahmoud, the articulate poet who gives voice to the millions displaced from their homelands.

Born in Darfur, Sudan Emi emigrated to Yemen and then the United States where she attended an Ivy League University. It was at Yale that she began to publicly compete in poetry 'slam' contests and eventually became the world champion. She used her pulpit to bring attention to the plight of refugees and to try to reconcile the civil battling forces within Darfur that made her family refugees in the first place.[4]

She has conferred with President Obama and the Dalai Lama, and represented Muslim and refugee perspectives in roundtable discussions, conferences and recited her poetry to the UN General Assembly. Her constituency are the tens of millions of refugees whom she represents as the UN High Commissioner for Refugees Goodwill Ambassador.

Here is an excerp from her award winning poem 'Mama.' You can see where she derives her strength.

"…Let me tell you something about my mama
She can reduce a man to tattered flesh without so much as blinking
Her words fester beneath your skin and the whole time,
You won't be able to stop cradling her eyes.
My mama is a woman, flawless and formidable in the same step.
Woman walks into a warzone and has warriors cowering at her feet
My mama carries all of us in her body,
on her face, in her blood and
Blood is no good once you let it loose
So she always holds us close.

When I was 7, she cradled bullets in the billows of her robes.
That same night, she taught me how to get gunpowder out of cotton with a bar of soap.
Years later when the soldiers held her at gunpoint and asked her who she was
She said, *I am a daughter of Adam, I am a woman, who the hell are you?*
The last time we went home, we watched our village burn,
Soldiers pouring blood from civilian skulls

---

[4] https://emi-mahmoud.com/

18

As if they too could turn water into wine.
They stole the ground beneath our feet.

The woman who raised me
turned and said, don't be scared
I'm your mother, I'm here, I won't let them through.
My mama gave me conviction.
Women like her
Inherit tired eyes,
Bruised wrists and titanium plated spines.
The daughters of widows wearing the wings of amputees
Carry countries between their shoulder blades…"

In 2018, she returned to Darfur, Sudan aided by Project Enough and began a 1000km (620 mile) walk across Sudan to engage people throughout the country in dialogue on how to bring peace to Sudan. It was unprecedented and people poured out into the streets wherever she went to meet her and engage with her. Her dedication and success caught the attention of the UNHCR. Soon she was appointed as Goodwill Ambassador for the UNHCR and travelled throughout the world to meet refugees, hear their stories and return to bring attention to their plight. She also founded a charity to help combat sickle cell in Nepal. She has stayed at refugee camps in Bangladesh, Cameroon, Jordan and Syria among many others.[5]

.

---

[5] https://www.unhcr.org/us/prominent-supporters/emtithal-mahmoud

CHAPTER 2: WOMEN LEADERS AT THE U.N. (UNITED NATIONS)

DR. ASHA-ROSE MIGIRO
Deputy Secretary General of the U.N. 2007 -2012.

An academic who transitioned into Law from her written work, she served on several legal reform commissions in Tanzania and at the United Nations. At the UN, she Chaired and Presided over committees and councils concerned with peace in the Great Lakes region of Africa. Her work included democracy-building in D.R. Congo. In Tanzania in the 2000s, she served as Foreign Minister with her concentration being the Great Lakes Region. Appointed Deputy Secretary General of the United Nations from 2007 – 2012, she concentrated on developing nations and gender discrimination and violence. She later ran for President of Tanzania in 2015, losing the nomination to the eventual winner of the election.[6]

---

[6] https://www.un.org/sg/en/content/asha-rose-migiro-former-deputy-secretary-general

SAHLE-WORK ZEWDE
President of Ethipia 2018 – present.
Former Under Secretary General of the U.N.

Sahle-Work was the second woman to be appointed as
Ambassador for Ethiopia, first in different stations and
accreditations in Africa in the 1990s and then to France in the early
2000s. From 2002 – 2006 she served as the Permanent

21

Representaqtive to UNESCO and her work began to transition to the UN sphere. In the late 2000s she headed the Peacebuilding UN mission in war torn Central African Republic until 2011, and the Director General of the UN Kenya office after that. [7]

2018 was an eventful year for her as .she was appointed Permanent Representative to the African Union in the rank of Under Secretary General of the UN, the first woman to hold that position. Just as she was looking forward to retiring a vacancy in the office of the Presidency of Ethiopia opend up and she was nominated and unanimously confirmed for the position in 2018. She will likely remain in that role for up to 12 years.[8] She is the first woman to serve in this capacity in Ethiopia.

During the Covid pandemic, she released 5500 prisoners from overcrowded prisons to slow the spread of the disease. She is actively working to end the Tigray War.

[7] https://en.wikipedia.org/wiki/Sahle-Work_Zewde
[8] https://en.wikipedia.org/wiki/Sahle-Work_Zewde

vi

KAMALA HARRIS
Vice-President of the U.S. 2021 – present.

Born to Jamaican Indian parents, Harris became a lawyer in the early 1990s and rose to serve as Deputy District Attorney, then DA in Oakland, CA then was elected Attorney General for the State of California in 2010, the first woman and first African American to hold that position. She was known as a tough prosecutor and took on gangs, drug trafficking and marijuana users. Her toughness served Californians well as she refused to settle with fraudulent national mortgage companies and the State was awarded a massive settlement as a result. Similarly she refused to cave in on pressure to support Proposition 8 which banned same-sex marriage and her steadfastness ultimately helped overturn the Proposition. She won election to the US Senate in 2015 running on a platform which included criminal justice reform, immigration reform and protection of a woman's right to choose. Her election was historical as she was the first Indian American and second African American woman elected to the Senate. She gained national attention for her speech at the Democratic National Convention and her grilling of high profile witnesses in the Russian 2016 Election interference hearings.

She ran for the Democratic Nomination for president in 2020, famously sparring with the eventual winner and nominee Joe Biden for his opposition to busing in the 1970s, when she spoke about the little kids being bused for fair and equitable access to schools, she famously said: "That little girl was me." It was a poignant moment for Biden and one he did not forget. Six months later he chose her as his running mate.[9]

The Biden administration has seen a contentious opposition and many issues came down to a single vote. Harris holds a tie for the record for the most tie-breaking Senate votes to pass legislation at 31 ties she has broken. In the US Senate, if there is a tie, the Vice President has the duty to break the tie. She has been a busy, high profile Vice President.[10]

---

[9] https://www.britannica.com/topic/vice-president-of-the-United-States-of-America

[10] https://en.wikipedia.org/wiki/List_of_tie-breaking_votes_cast_by_the_vice_president_of_the_United_States

vii

AOC
ALEXANDRIA OCASIO-CORTEZ
Creator of the Green New Deal U.S Congress
House Leader of the U.S Social-Democrats

Rarely is a politician so well known that everyone knows them by their initials. There are only a handful of examples and, except RBG, all are men: JFK, LBJ, RFK, X. Alexandria Ocasio Cortez, known widely as AOC is a mould-breaking politician. Elected the youngest Woman in the history of the U.S to Congress, having served as a waiter, a bartender and Educational Director for the National

Hispanic Institute recently before her election. She served as a Community organizer for Bernie Sanders in his 2016 bid for the White House. [11] Her life experiences, the Sanders campaign and the example of other activists motivated her to run for a difficult seat for Congress. Outspent 10 to 1, up against a 20 year incumbent, she shocked the political world with a 13% win. She brought a fearless social-democratic sensibility to the House, boldly arriving with a Green New Deal to directly take on the special oil and gas interests and combat global warming. Though much of her party's senior leadership seemed to dismiss the wide reaching ambitious plan, much of what she proposed was later co-opted by the Biden Administrations Inflation Reduction Act, so named to deflect its Green New Deal roots. She fiercely protects the rights of average Americans and holds powerful interests accountable when she grills them in Congressional Hearings. She and her mentor Bernie Sanders represent the leadership of the Progressive or Social Democratic wing of the Democratic party.

Her hardworking backstory began when he father died as she attended Boston College. She and her mother scrambled to pay the medical bills and not lose the house. When she visited Standing Rock Indian protests and she saw people who were willing to sacrifice for their cause, she decided to join the world of politics. Today, she and a small group of progressive Congresswomen are known as 'the Squad.' They speak truth to power, fight fervently for average Americans and Immigrants and have redefined what it is to be a principled American politician – they are young and all female. To date, she has sponsored 15 Bills which are now laws on housing, workers protection, anti-poverty, a ban on fracking, corporate accountability, environmental protections, the prohibition of police to use chemical weapons, and financial relief during Covid. [12]

---

[11] Educational Director for the National Hispanic Institute
[12] Projects.propublica.org

NANCY PELOSI
Speaker of the U.S House 2007 – 2011, 2019 – 2023.

Pelosi was born to a powerful Baltimore political family, with her father serving as Mayor and Congressman from the City. When she graduated from College she married and moved to San Francisco where she became involved in local politics. In 1987 she won election to the US House of Representatives from her adopted home. Always on the vanguard of GLBTA politics, the savvy Pelosi ascended into the Democratic Party leadership as Democratic Whip in the House in 2001, a high profile position which showcased her leadership and political instincts. The following year, she was elected Democratic Leader, becoming the first woman in US history to do so. As Leader and then when the Democrats were in the majority as Speaker of the House, from 2007 - 2011, and again from 2019 - 2023 she ushered in significant and impactful legislation including laws that protected women from discrimination, the Affordable Care Act, environmental protections and aid for students attending college.[13] Her nearly two decade tenure set a record as the longest a Democratic leader had ever served at the helm.[14] She famously gave the smallest of sardonic claps as she stood behind Mr. Trump during his State of the Union speech. It was a simple but powerful gesture that had the nations forget the speech and talk about Pelosi.

The divisiveness of the Trump-era politics spilled over into the Biden Presidency and Pelosi's home was invaded by a hammer wielding assailant to attacked her husband but was there to attack her. After stepping down from the Speaker position, she remained in the House representing San Francisco.

---

[13] https://www.womenofthehall.org/inductee/nancy-pelosi/
[14] https://abcnews.go.com/Politics/nancy-pelosis-accomplishments-controversies-house-leadership/story?id=93502266

HILLARY CLINTON
1st Woman to Win the U.S Presidential Popular Vote
1st American Women Candidate to Win a Major Party
Nomination, 2016.

*"Despite all the challenges we face, I remain
convinced that the future is female."*

Hillary Clinton won the 2016 U.S Presidential election popular vote
by three million votes. [ix] The President of the United States is chosen,
however, by a system called the Electoral College (EC), which was
designed to give smaller American states a bigger influence than is

proportionate to their populations. Otherwise the smaller states might be ignored in the general election. In the Electoral College, she received 232 votes to 306 for Donald Trump.ˣ It takes 270 Electoral College to become President.

Clinton was a successful lawyer who defended the rights of women and children, prior to becoming First Lady of the U.S state of Arkansas (her husband Bill Clinton was the state's governor). Bill Clinton won the U.S Presidency in 1992 and again in 1996, with Hillary serving as First Lady of the U.S, she championed Universal Health Care, which was defeated in Congress. Hillary wielded power and influence in her own right within the Clinton Administration, so much so that after Bill retired from politics, she ran and won the vacated New York Senate seat. After a successful career in the U.S Senate, she ran for President and was heavily favored to win the Democratic nomination against freshman Senator Barack Obama. When Obama won the upset victory in 2008, Clinton served as Obama's Secretary of State, which she did with distinction. Hillary ran for President again in 2016 with mixed results. After beating back an impressive challenge from Democratic/Socialist Senator Bernie Sanders, she was again heavily favored to win against controversial Republican candidate Trump.

There had been wide expectation across the United States, in the media and in both political parties that Clinton would win. Her defeat will go down as one of the most surprising election results in U.S. history. In the last weeks of the campaign, the government of Russia hacked her party and her campaign email. They published embarrassing messages which showed the DNC had breached its neutrality by supporting her over Senator Sanders in the primaries. Additionally, embarrassing emails from her campaign manager were released which reduced her lead in the final days of the campaign. Also in the last week, FBI Director Comey launched a baseless criminal investigation of Clinton's email leaked by the Russians. The unprecedented Russian and FBI election interference likely changed the election result. An investigation is currently underway into whether Trump and his campaign colluded illegally with the Russians to win the election. While Hillary Clinton was not elected President of the United States, it is important to recognize the glass ceilings she *has* broken and influence Clinton she *has* wielded. Here are a few of Hillary Clinton's achievements to date:

➢ Won the popular vote in the 2016 U.S Presidential Election.
➢ The first woman to serve as a major U.S Party's nominee for President of the United States.
➢ The first woman U.S Senator from the State of New York.
➢ The first, First Lady to run for elective office and win.
➢ The second woman to serve as U.S Secretary of State.
➢ The first woman to receive a significant number of delegates in any major U.S. political party in the nominating contest for President (2008).
➢ Served as First Lady of the United States, 1992 – 2000.
➢ Led the first U.S national effort for Universal Healthcare.
➢ The first women partner in the Rosewater Law Firm.

ALEQA HAMMOND
1st Woman Prime Minister of Greenland
(Kalaallit Nunaat) 2013 – 2014.

"Greenlanders' heart is the environment. You can't sell your heart for oil."

Aleqa Hammond is a Member of the Danish Parliament who ran for PM of Greenland, an autonomous Republic administered by Denmark. She grew up in a town of 1400 in western Greenland. Elected to the Greenland Parliament, she has been a proponent of Greenland's independence.[xi] She campaigned on the idea of lifting the uranium-extraction ban to help her country's mining industry. [xii] She won the election and her uranium mining bill became law. In 2014 she stepped down as Prime Minister because of financial irregularities. [xiii]

xiv

KIM CAMPBELL
1st Woman Prime Minister of Canada, 1993.

"I have always believed governments must adapt to the needs of the people, not the other way around."

Campbell began her political career as the first female President of her High School. She worked in the Vancouver School Board and in local politics. In 1988 she was elected to the Canadian Parliament and in 1989 she received her first Ministerial appointment for Indian Affairs. From 1990 - 1993 she was Minister of Justice and Attorney General for Canada. She reformed the legal codes effecting gun control and sexual assault crimes. She became Minister of National Defense in 1993, as Canadian Prime Minister Mulroney retired.[xv] She quickly solidified support and won election to finish the four months left in his term. Her style was blunt and honest and was appreciated by voters at first. But by election time, voters had tired of pessimism and sought solutions which she didn't seem to have. [xvi] [xvii] [15]

[15] https://www.globalspeakers.com/speakers/kim-campbell/

Women
and the
Presidency

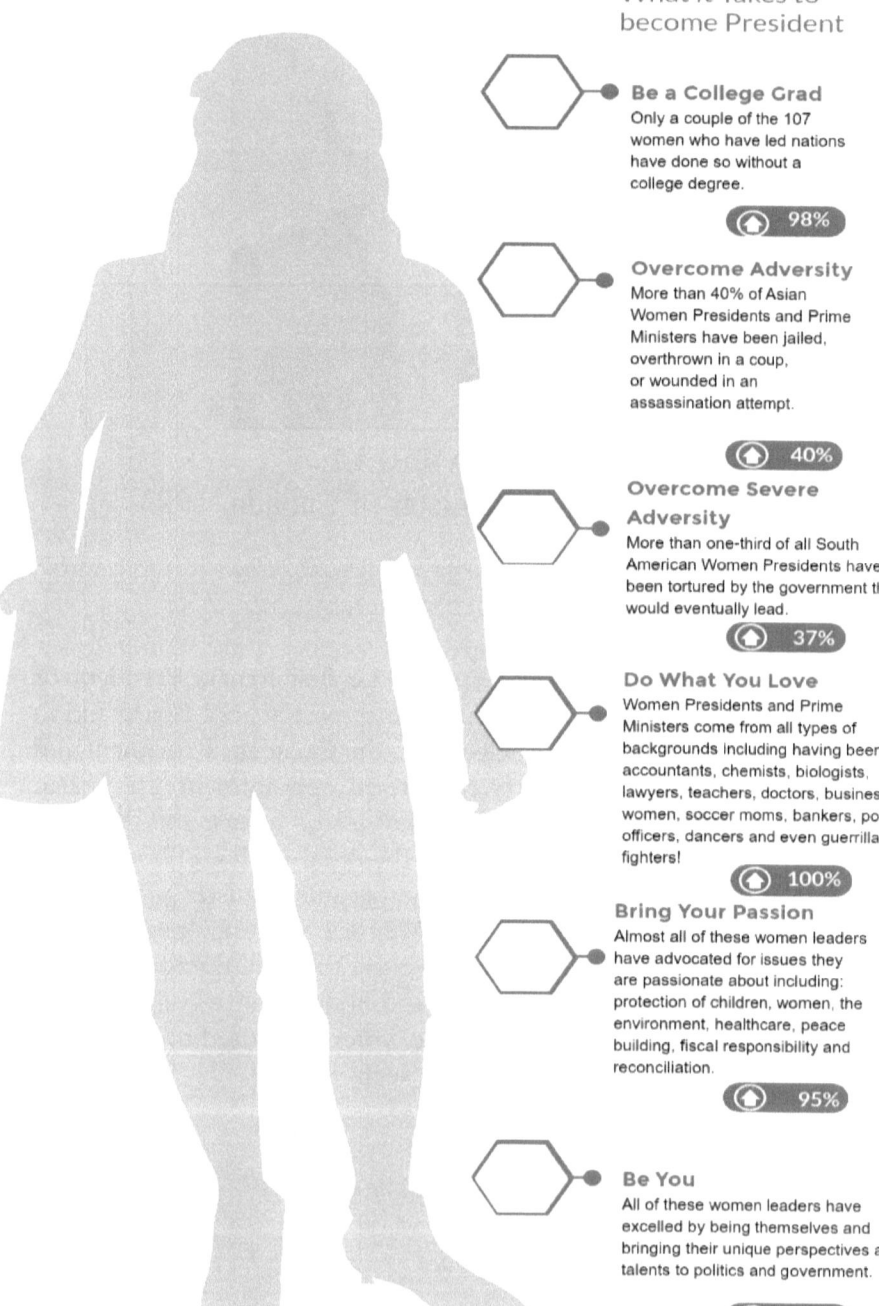

What it Takes to become President

Be a College Grad
Only a couple of the 107 women who have led nations have done so without a college degree.

⬆ 98%

Overcome Adversity
More than 40% of Asian Women Presidents and Prime Ministers have been jailed, overthrown in a coup, or wounded in an assassination attempt.

⬆ 40%

Overcome Severe Adversity
More than one-third of all South American Women Presidents have been tortured by the government they would eventually lead.

⬆ 37%

Do What You Love
Women Presidents and Prime Ministers come from all types of backgrounds including having been accountants, chemists, biologists, lawyers, teachers, doctors, business women, soccer moms, bankers, police officers, dancers and even guerrilla fighters!

⬆ 100%

Bring Your Passion
Almost all of these women leaders have advocated for issues they are passionate about including: protection of children, women, the environment, healthcare, peace building, fiscal responsibility and reconciliation.

⬆ 95%

Be You
All of these women leaders have excelled by being themselves and bringing their unique perspectives and talents to politics and government.

⬆ 100%

XIOMARA CASTRO
1st Woman President of Honduras 2022 – present.

Castro served as the First lady of Honduras from 2006 – 200 until her husband, then President Manuel Zelaya, was overthrown in a military coup. She led the street protests and massive movement against the coup. She rose to lead the LIBRE party and stood as its nominee for President in 2013 polling second. She was on the losing side of the 2017 ticket as well, in each case with voting irregularities and suspicious blackouts which led to their ticket losing what looked like a sure victory. Finally in 2021, she was elected President in her own right, the first woman President of Honduras. When her coalition was victorious in 2022 she moved to make good on a promise to her running mates party. She had made an agreement with her running mate Salvador Nasralla who had headed their 2017 ticket as the Candidate for President, and she Vice President. He woiuld not seek the Presidency in 2022, but his Party would be given the leadership of Congress. When 20 members of her own Party LIBRE broke that promise and tried to install someone else, she denounced and expelled them from the party and decried the attempt to kidnap the election. Her integrity and forcefulness pressured the twenty into abandoning their effort in exchange for forgiveness and readmission into the LIBRE Party. Order was restored.

However order was not restored to the Country of Honduras which has one of the world's highest crime rates including crimes against women.[16] Rather than continue the cycle of corruption in the Justice system she invited the UN to develop an International Commission to fight corruption.[17] She passed laws cutting down on pollution, and gave free electricity to the nation's poorest, and protected Indigenous Tribes who were being harassed. She is fighting for more transparency at every level of government. Honduras remains a violent and dangerous nation, but is slowly seems to be heading in the right direction under Castro's leadership.

---

[16] https://www.wola.org/analysis/xiomara-castro-expectations-challenges-pending-debts/

[17] https://en.wikipedia.org/wiki/Xiomara_Castro

PORTIA SIMPSON-MILLER
1st Woman Prime Minister of Jamaica
2006 – 2007, 2012 – 2016.

Mrs. Simpson Miller served for nearly 20 years in various Cabinet Minister positions including Labor, Social Security and Sport; Tourism, Entertainment, Local Government, Community Development and Women's Affairs. Known as 'Sister P' or 'Mama P,' the popular Simpson-Miller was first elected Prime Minister in 2006, but her party was defeated which removed her from leadership. Re-elected in 2012, Simpson-Miller served four as PM. [xx] During her term, she was responsible for:

- ➢ Strengthened national insurance protection.
- ➢ Advocated for equality of the LGBT community. [xxi]

[xxii]LAURA CHINCHILLA
1st Woman President of Costa Rica
2010 – 2014.

"The internet is the hope of an integrated world without frontiers, a common world without controlling owners, a world of opportunities and equality. This is a utopia that we have been dreaming about and is the world in which each and every one of us are protagonists of a destiny we have in our hands."

The safety of Costa Ricans, women and the vulnerable around the world have always been a top priority for Georgetown University educated Laura Chinchilla. She was the first woman elevated to become Minister of Public Security in 1996. Her many achievements include making the Costa Rican police more professional, reforming the criminal codes to make them more fair, adopting laws against drug trafficking and citizen crime-prevention initiatives. Elected to Congress in 2002, she chaired the Committee on Legal Affairs and the Committee on Narcotics. [xxiii] [xxiv]

After working as both the Vice President and the Minister of Justice, she was elected President in 2010. She served her full term and her achievements highlight her priorities. During her term, she:

- ➢ Decreased crime, homicide and femicide.
- ➢ Promoted women's rights and children's rights. [xxv]
- ➢ Promoted environmental protection (she received 2 awards).

After her term, she has kept a high international profile continuing to work and teach on these issues. [xxvi] She later returned to Georgetown University as a Fellow in the Institute of Politics and Public Service. [xxvii]

xxviii

MICHELE PIERRE-LOUIS
President of Haiti 2008 – 2009

"Haitians have shown tremendous energy and such an incredible desire to be enfranchised. It would be a shame if we did not build on this energy and build a new Haiti."[xxix]

Pierre-Louise was educated in economics at Queen's College in NY. She became a well-known advocate in Haiti on a variety of social and educational issues. In 1991, she served in President Aristide's Cabinet in several capacities often as a liaison between the President and the Ministries. [xxx] She worked with the Foundation of Knowledge and Freedom from 1995 – 2008 and served as Minister of Justice. Pierre-Louis became the second woman Prime Minister of Haiti when two other candidates failed to be confirmed. A sluggish economy and no discernable progress lead to her government being dissolved. Upon leaving office in November 2009, she returned and coordinated special post-earthquake reconstruction projects. [xxxi]

MIREYA DE ARIAS
1st Woman President of Panama 1999 – 2004.

"I want for this country what I want for my son Ricardo that he has the right to grow up in a democratic country, with guaranteed freedoms, with judicial stability and with social justice."

Mireya de Arias grew up in poverty in Panama and met the President of Panama at a party when she was 17 years old. She worked in his coffee business and in his political campaigns. He was re-elected President and was overthrown in a coup against his government. She joined Arras in exile and they were married a year later. Even though she was 43 years his junior, they were together for 20 years. She learned how to run political campaigns and the government of Panama. When asked about her lack of education, she responded:

"My biggest University was that of Dr. Arias."

When he died, she returned to Panama and was approached to take up his leadership position. She refused at first. But in time she agreed to become involved in politics and in 1991 she took the reins of Arras's political party. In 1994, she ran a close election for President but lost. In 1998, her campaign was successful. During her Presidential term, the highlights were, she:

➢ Supervised the Canal transfer from the U.S to Panama.
➢ Supervised U.S troops exit from Panama.
➢ Decreased unemployment.

Upon exiting the office, she called sexism the biggest obstacle of her political career. [xxxii]

VIOLETA DE CHAMORRO
1st Woman President in Central America & Nicaragua
1990 – 1996

"Reconciliation is more beautiful than victory."

In the early 1950s, Violeta de Chamorro married her husband who was a newspaper editor of the leftist newspaper *La Prenza*. His paper was very critical of the Somoza dictatorship which led to their exile in 1957. For the next twenty years, he (they) remained critical of Somoza. Pedro, her husband, was imprisoned several times and was assassinated by the dictatorship in 1978. His death sparked a revolution that overthrew Somoza and installed the Marxist Sandinistas. [xxxiv]

De Chamorro continued in the Sandinista leadership and took over his newspaper. She became a critic of the Sandinistas and her newspaper was often censored and finally shut down for two years.

43

In 1990, a long-standing guerilla war was brought to a peaceful conclusion and Nicaragua had their first free election. De Chamorro led a 14-political party coalition to oppose the Sandinista incumbent Daniel Ortega. She won a surprisingly strong victory and became, not only the first woman President in Nicaragua, but the first to be elected in Central America.

This is what national reconciliation looks like.
Ortega and De Chamorro genuinely reconcile.

As President, she was known for:

> ➤ Lifting censorship of the media.
> ➤ Privatizing state owned industries.
> ➤ Reducing the size and budget of the military. [xxxv]
> ➤ Helping negotiate final terms of the peace. [xxxvi]
> ➤ She did not run for a 2nd term.

CLAUDETTE WERLEIGH
1st Woman Prime Minister of Haiti 1995 - 1996.

"It's only when the interests of one country coincide with the interests of another that things work."[xxxviii]

Claudette Werleigh came from a coffee exporting family and her father was a Member of Parliament. During her career, she worked in a variety of jobs around the world. In the late 1960s, she worked in the United States as a chemist, in the early 1970s as a Physiologist in Switzerland and a teacher in Haiti before practicing law. [xxxix]

Her husband was involved in Haitian politics and he introduced Werleigh to yet another career. While practicing law, Werleigh also helped local NGOs in their humanitarian work on the island nation. For over a decade she worked in Haiti and throughout the Caribbean for Caritas International, a humanitarian aid group. She also founded schools and women's organizations. So, by the time she was ready to enter politics, Werleigh was known to many Haitians. In 1990, she served as Minister of Social Affairs in Pascal-Trouillot's interim Presidency. She returned to the Cabinet in 1993 as Minister of Foreign Affairs and was drafted to serve as Prime Minister in 1995 – 1996. Werleigh served for a few months to organize a free and fair election and oversee the successful transition to a new democratic government. [xl] Which she did, successfully.

She accomplished a great deal in the few months she was in office, including receiving financial support for several Haitian projects and improving ties with her neighbors. The new President wished to keep her on as Prime Minister but could not due to political alliances in the Parliament. She stepped down and chose to work outside of Haiti. [xli] She has held two high profile positions since leaving as Prime Minister. She has served as Director of the Life and Peace Institute in Uppsala, Sweden. And she also has served as Peace Envoy and Chair for Pax Christi International. [xlii]

DAME EUGENIA CHARLES
1st Woman Prime Minister of Dominica 1980 – 1995.

Eugenia Charles attended a convent boarding school as a girl and University of Toronto and the London School of Economics as an adult. After completing her studies in law and economics, Charles became the first woman in Dominica to practice law. When the ruling party of the soon to be independent island nation attempted to pass a bill to repress the opposition, known as the "shut your mouth" bill, she became politically active. She helped form the Dominica Freedom Party in 1968 and entered Assembly House as a Representative in 1970. Early in her career she created a stir by arriving to Parliament in a bathing suit to protest a proposed dress code. She rose to become a Member of Parliament in 1975. [xliv] She was sober, argued very well and was seen as a steadfast and stable leader when she was elevated to Prime Minister in 1980. Known as 'Mamo' to the people she represented, Eugenia Charles survived coup attempts by remaining level-headed. During one attempted coup, she calmly walked to the front door, locked it and calmly walked out the back door to safety as the coup plotters tried to enter the front.

The United States invasion of the small Caribbean Island of Grenada was done at the request of Charles after Grenada's President Bishop had been killed in a coup.

In her third and final term, she began to be viewed as out of touch by many citizens. [xlv] [xlvi]

The major accomplishments of her terms were:

➤ Electricity was connected throughout Dominica.
➤ Road paving was completed throughout the island and infrastructure was improved.
➤ Dominica became stable and had good relations with US.

Despite her down to earth, no-frills, schoolmarm style, many of the poor saw her failure to reduce discrimination and poverty as big flaws. *"During her years in office, she would see constituents and visitors in her modest office or on the sweeping verandah of her family home, she would sit in a battered wooden chair, her shoes kicked off, watching a miniature TV set and eating chunks of sugarcane."* [xlvii] Retiring as Prime Minister in 1995, she went on to monitor elections around the world for the Carter Center. [xlviii] She was unmarried with no children.

xlix

MICHELLE BACHELET
1st Woman President Chile 2006 - 2010, 2014 - Present

"My message to women is: We can do it. We are capable of doing almost anything, but we must learn we cannot do it all at once, prioritize."

Michelle Bachelet's father, an Air Force general, was tortured to death by the Pinochet regime. As a medical student, Michelle was also tortured and when she was released, she went into exile until the dictator Pinochet retired. [1] Before her political ascent, Bachelet was a Pediatrician and a human rights activist. She served as Health Minister and then Defense Minister for Chile. [li] She has accomplished the rare feat of being elected President in two non-consecutive terms. In her first term 2006 - 2010, she was widely credited for preventing the world economic

meltdown from effecting Chile. Despite this, she was voted out, only to stage a political comeback in 2014. In her second term, she is seeking to rewrite the old Constitution which dates back to the dictatorship. She also seeks to raise taxes on corporations and increase access to higher education. [lii]

"My father respected and admired my mother and was a person who was always standing by my side, encouraging me to do more and believed in my capacity. So, in that sense, my own experience was very good in becoming an empowered woman. From early on, I carried that strong message."

liii

DILMA ROUSSEFF
1st Woman President of Brazil
2011 – 2016.

"This was a Parliamentary coup. No one is saying we did not commit mistakes. We did. It would be absurd to say we were committed no mistakes, But we won four elections. The Brazilian people knew what they were voting for. But this wasn't in line with the individuals who led the coup."4/17[liv]

Rousseff started her political career as a Marxist guerrilla in the 1970s against Brazil's brutal military dictatorship. Her *nom de guerre* name was 'Estela.' She was captured and savagely beaten and tortured. She was given electric shock, upside down suspension, and beatings that broke her teeth and shifted her dental ridge.

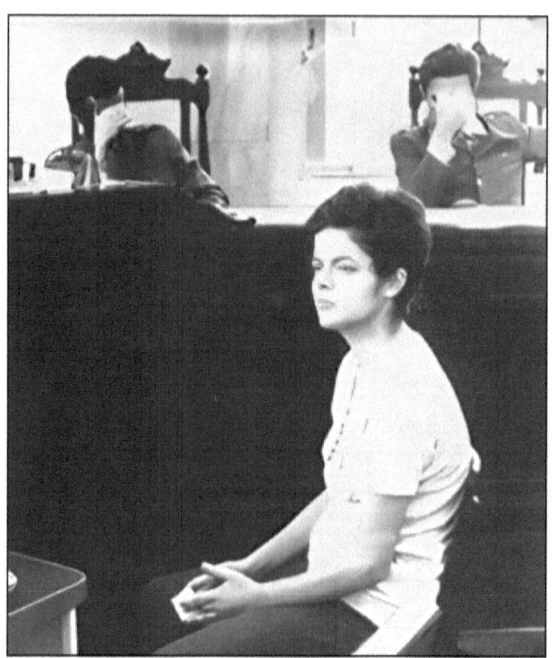
Rousseff's trial as a captured guerilla fighter.[lv]

In the 1980s when Brazil became a democracy, Rousseff studied and took part in local politics. [lvi] She was promoted to Energy Minister and Chief of Staff to the very popular President Lula da Silva. Da Silva presided over Brazil's 'economic miracle' which saw Brazil pay off all its international debt. When he was term-limited out, Rousseff was chosen to lead Brazil.

During her first term, Rousseff remained very popular and the economy continued to be strong. But as the economy slowed, several issues she championed such as the new hydro-electric dams proved to be unpopular with the people they displaced. Constituencies which would normally be warm to her leftist views, such as the GLBT community, felt overlooked by her administration. The end of her first term and the beginning of her second were very rocky with massive protests and accusations of corruption. In 2016, she was impeached and removed from office by the Senate. It is widely acknowledged that she accepted no bribes, though graft have occurred in the state-owned gas company she administered.[lvii]

CRISTINA FERNANDEZ DE KIRCHNER
President of Argentina 2007 – 2015.

"Empowering women should not be just a matter of obligation (by governments), but a personal conviction by men and ourselves. We need to break the cultural barriers that historically consider women to be inferior to men."

Fernandez de Kirchner met her husband, future Argentine President Nestor Kirchner in College. [lix] After College they fled the upheaval to Kirchner's hometown and opened a law practice together. When the dictatorship ended, they were both elected to office. She was elected to the local legislature and he as Mayor of his hometown. They both had parallel political careers, he rising to serve as Governor of the Province of Santa Cruz and she being elected to the National Senate.

Though both were Peronists (right of center – named after former dictator Peron), Fernandez became one of the nation's leading critics of the Menem, the Peronist President. In 2003, weakened from her attacks, Menem withdrew from the runoff against her husband. Kirchner became President of Argentina and Fernandez, the country's first lady.

Nestor Kirchner served one term which was dominated by Argentina's economic turbulence and he did not run for re-election. Cristina Fernandez Kirchner ran instead and was elected President of Argentina in 2007. Nestor died of a heart attack in 2010. [lx]

A young glamour shot, husband Kirchner's big victory. [lxi lxii]

Seeking to stabilize the economy and make it more equitable she proposed a new tax system which was rejected. She then nationalized private pension funds, fired the Director of the Central Bank and nationalized YPF energy firm. Argentina did default on its debts in her second term, Fernandez defended her decision to default by saying this:

"Debts should be honored but not if it starves people." [lxiii]

She placed better currency control mechanisms to help regulate the currency and money value fluctuation. She and her administration were accused of corruption and during her attempt to amend the Constitution to allow her to run for a third term, her party was soundly defeated, ending her term. [lxiv]

JANET JAGAN
1st Woman President & Prime Minister of Guyana
1997 – 1999

"Nothing much frightens me."[lxvi]

Janet Jagan moved to Guyana from the U.S with her Guyanese husband, Cheddi, in 1943. She was stripped of her U.S citizenship because of her Marxist convictions. She helped her husband with his dental practice and founded a women's organization in the 1940s in Guyana. In 1950, the couple was instrumental in the establishment of the People's Progressive Party. Janet chaired the party for the next twenty years. Their platform was very left of center and promoted the independence of Guyana from Britain. They won the Parliamentary elections of 1953 and her husband, Cheddi, was appointed Prime Minister (though still a British colony). But his

government was dismissed less than a half a year into its term by the British who feared the prospect of both the island's independence movement and their leftist outlook. In 1955 Janet and Cheddi were jailed for their political views. In the 1957 election, their party won again and Cheddi was re-appointed Prime Minister and Janet, Minister of Labor. [lxvii] The years that followed were turbulent. There was violence and instability in Guyana. Despite this, they made some improvements to everyday life. In 1966, Guyana achieved Independence from Great Britain. Jagan became the editor of the *Mirror* newspaper and founded a journalist union. She served as a Member of Parliament from the 1970s – 1980s. [lxviii]

Cheddi was President from 1992 – 1997 and suffered a fatal heart attack in 1997. He is widely considered to be the father of Guyana. Janet Jagan was elevated to become the country's first female Vice-President and Prime Minister. She also became the PPP's candidate for the 1997 elections. After winning, Jagan became the first female President of Guyana. She also received the Gandhi Gold Medal for Peace from U.N.E.S.C.O. She resigned in 1999 for health reasons, Jagan remained an active member of the PPP. [lxix] Jagan is the first American-born woman to serve as the President of an independent nation.

LIDIA TEJADA
1st Woman President of Bolivia
1979 – 1980.

As a student, Lidia Tejada had studied in the 1940s to become an accountant. But she soon led a life of political revolt and service. Her first widely acclaimed experience came in 1951 when she led a hunger strike of 26 women over 8 days to successfully free political prisoners. She helped lead protests which overthrew the 1952 dictatorship.[lxx] She joined the MNR Party and when they came to power in 1952, she became a Congresswoman. When her party's government was overthrown, she was subsequently detained and tortured. She fled the country in 1964. When she returned in 1979, she rose to become President of Parliament.

In 1979, when another military coup overthrew the President, the coup plotters failed to remain in power. Tejada was elevated to the vacant Presidency by succession by virtue of her position as President of the Parliament. She served for eight months as Interim President to restore a democratically elected government. As Tejada assumed office, hopes were high that she could lead the nation to a fair and free election. She did. The election was held, but the transition never occurred, because within two weeks of the election, the military overthrew her in a bloody coup before the elected government could be sworn in. For one shining moment, a woman had broken through the ultimate glass ceiling in Bolivia. [lxxii] She lived in exile in France until 1982 when the Bolivian dictatorship fell, she returned and served as an Ambassador for Bolivia and worked in several feminist organizations. [lxxiii] She was the cousin of Rachel Welch, the actress was born Tejada. Ironically it was another cousin, General Luis Tejada, who overthrew her. He was jailed after the coup and remains there today.

CAREER

paths for women

to become President or Prime Minister

01

Lawyer
The most common career path for men and women, alike, to become leader of their respective nations is still the law.

02

Politics
Local elected office, staff, campaigns, media, fundraising and all things political.

03

Government
Working in a local, state or national agency, department or administration can lead to a elected career.

04

Teacher
Aside from the standard career choices of law and politics, teaching heads the list. It combines knowledge, public speaking and leadership.

05

Accountant/Economist
Economic and financial affairs are all-important in business and life; it's no different in politics.

06

Scientist (chemist/biologist)
From finding plant-based cures for cancer, to global warming solution, science is a surprising new career path to national leadership.

07

Manager/Administrator
High level corporate management and University administration are top backgrounds for a transition to politics.

08

Stay-at-Home-Mom
Women have recently ascended to the highest office in the land. How different is running a family than a country?

09

Guerilla Fighter/Revolutionary
Believe it or not, several women including former President Dilma Rousseff of Brazil got their political start in an armed revolution.

10

Doctor/Engineer/Business/Reporter
This 4-way tie between very different career paths highlights how varied the backgrounds of todays women leaders are.

lxxiv

VICTOIRE TOMEGAH DOGBE
1st Female Prime Minister of Togo 2020 – present.

Victoire Dogbe's appointment as the first woman Prime Minister of Togo was seen as a victory for competent women in Togo and elsewhere. Dogbe was a widely respected Cabinet Minister and Chief of Staff to the President.[18] She had previously worked for the UN Development Program and brings an organized focus to employment and economy generating policies.[19] International Organizations are comfortable with her at or near the helm for Togo's economy.

---

[18] https://thewomenleaders.com/victoire-tomegah-dogbe/
[19] https://www.cnn.com/2020/09/29/africa/togo-female-prime-minister-intl/index.html

NADJE ROMDHANE
1st Female Prime Minister of Tunisia 2021 – 2023.

In a surprising move, the controversial President of Tunisia who seized power for himself and sacked the last Prime Minister, appointed a relative political novice in Nadje Romdhame, an engineer and geologist by training. The teacher had brief experience with a temporary Cabinet portfolio prior to the appointment. Her ascension marks the first time a woman has held this position in Tunisia. The question remains, will she be a breath of fresh air or simply a distraction to take focus off of the power grab. The President will retain the vast majority of powers despite asking her to form a government.[20]

---

[20] https://www.aljazeera.com/news/2021/9/29/who-is-najla-romdhane-tunisias-first-female-prime-minister

SAMIA SULUHU HASSAN
President of Tanzania 2021 – Present.

"The opposition is lucky that it is a woman president in charge because if a misunderstanding occurs, I will stand for peace and make the men settle their egos,"[21]

Hassan began her storied political career in Zanzibar in 2000, since then she served in a variety of elected and appointed political offices. In 2014, she was elected Vice-President of the Constitutional Assembly to write a new Constitution for Tanzania.[22] She served as Vice President and became President by ascension. She lifted a ban on political rallies and freed political opposition leaders and allowed more freedom in the press. [23] [24]

[21] https://apnews.com/article/international-womens-day-tanzania-samia-suluhu-hassan-africa-democracy-a4215c9574269a0832612d264e667aaf

[22] http://sheisafrica.eu/2021/06/29/women-presidents-in-africa-2/

[23] https://apnews.com/article/international-womens-day-tanzania-samia-suluhu-hassan-africa-democracy-a4215c9574269a0832612d264e667aaf

ROSE RAPONDA
Prime Minister of Gabon 2020 – 2023.
Vice President 2023 – present.

Raponda studied economics and worked her way to head the Housing Bank of Gabon, and budget Minister of Gabon from 2012 - 2014, then was elected Mayor of the nation's capital from 2014 -2019, when she was elevated to Defense Minister. When the PM stepped down, she was seen as a stabilizing and unifying force and was asked to serve out his term.[25] She was recently appointed to the position of Vice-President after her term as PM was over.

---

[24] https://www.britannica.com/biography/Samia-Suluhu-Hassan
[25] https://thewomenleaders.com/rose-christiane-raponda/

ELLEN JOHNSON SIRLEAF
1st Female Elected Head of State in Africa
1st Female President of Liberia 2006 -2018.

"If your dreams do not scare you,
they are not big enough"

Ellen Johnson Sirleaf was born in Monrovia, Liberia. Her father was the first indigenous member of the Liberian Assembly. She was married at 17 years of age and was a homemaker to her four children and a bookkeeper for an auto repair shop. After travelling with her husband to the U.S, she received her Finance Degree from Madison Business College in Wisconsin. After she and her husband divorced, Sirleaf began working in Liberia's Ministry of Finance.

As she rose through the ranks to become the Assistant Minister of Finance, she became well known for her strong call against corporate hoarding of Liberian wealth and resources. [lxxvii] She lost her job as Assistant Minister due to her political views but six years later, in 1979, she became the Finance Minister of Liberia.

In 1980, a violent coup led by Samuel Doe overthrew the government and executed most of the sitting government leadership. Sirleaf's life was spared and she was offered a position in Samuel Doe's new government. Rather than accept the position, she fled to the United States, where she worked for the World Bank. [lxxviii]

In 1985 she returned to Liberia to run for Vice President and was jailed for her fiery speeches. Excluded from the ticket, she ran and was elected to the Liberian Senate. Again, she refused to serve due to the perception of widespread voter fraud during the election. After the election, she was briefly arrested twice and defiantly continued her opposition work until she was forced to flee again to the U.S. [lxxix]

During this time she worked as the Director of the United Nations Development Program Regional Bureau for Africa. But eventually returned to Liberian politics. Liberian dictator Charles Taylor was coming to power. She initially supported Taylor, but that support was short lived as she soon realized his intensions. Sirleaf opposed him in the 1997 election for President receiving 25% of the vote to his 75%, in what was largely seen as a fraudulent election. Again Sirleaf was accused of treason and fled to Ivory Coast after the election. [lxxx]

lxxxi

Young Sirleaf defiant after release from prison.

After the end of the second Liberian Civil War and the conviction of Charles Taylor for 'Crimes against Humanity,' Sirleaf ran and won the Presidency in 2005. In the next election, she won a lopsided victory shortly after being awarded the Nobel Peace Prize for leading her nation's peaceful reconciliation. As President, she has:

> Made education compulsory and free for all elementary school children
> Significantly reduced and negotiated down Liberia's national debt, in some cases discounted by up to 97%.
> Created the Freedom of Information Act to make government transparent to guard against corruption.
> Championed the protection of gay rights, which is rare in Africa.

Sirleaf's second term ended in January 2018. She has ten grandchildren. For fun, she once announced the arrest of the political opposition as an April Fools' joke.

AMEENAH GURIB-FAKIM
President Mauritius 2015 -2018.

"I've gone through the glass ceiling, that's an important message to send to young women and girls."

Ameenah Gurib-Fakim is an organic chemist who was drafted to become the President of the Mauritius. She taught organic chemistry as a professor in the University of Mauritius, founded a research center and received widespread acclaim after her TED-lecture presentation on healing plant life and her work for the World Bank. During a political impasse when the sitting President and his party attempted to redraft the Constitution to extend his term, Gurib-Fakim was asked to stand for election. Her clean political slate and dedication to the environment of Mauritius made her an easy favorite and she was elected in June of 2015. She felt that the opportunity to work as President would yield a rare chance to

---

[26] Public Domain. https://globalvoices.org/2015/07/01/africa-celebrates-renowned-scientist-ameenah-gurib-fakim-as-mauritius-first-female-president/

advocate against global warming and bring attention to the healing potential of some of Mauritius' flora and fauna.

"For a long time, people were suspicious of the "bad plants" that I was studying for their medical properties. Some called me "witch", and at night 20 years ago, my lab was burned down."

She grew from a nature-loving child, to a Medical Center Director to create cures from the flora and fauna she loved, to the leader of her island nation.

One of her best-known claims is that plant life on Mauritius and elsewhere in the India Ocean may be able to combat bacteria as a natural alternative to antibiotics. She contends that the Baume de l'lle plate can offer an alternative treatment for asthma and proposes that the Boabab tree should be used as a food source for babies because it has more protein than human milk. [lxxxiii]

She has broken many glass ceilings in her career; she was the first female professor at the University of Mauritius, the first female Dean of the Faculty of Science, the first female founder of a research center on Mauritius and, of course, the first elected female President of Mauritius. Unfortunately, credit card irregularities ended her term as President. She has not been charged with wrongdoing.

SAARA KUUGONGELWA
First Woman Prime Minister of Namibia 2015 - Present

"Women's rights are human rights."

Saara Kuugongelwa went into exile from Namibia at the young age of 13 due to political and civil unrest related to the SWAPO independence movement. Namibia was the scene of a proxy war between the USSR and the US, with SWAPO aligned with the Soviet Union. [lxxxiv] She was educated in Sierra Leone and received a BS in Economics at Lincoln University in the U.S. Upon returning to Namibia, she served in the Office of the President Nujoma.

70

After making a good impression in the President's Office, Kuugongelwa was appointed Director of the National Planning Commission for Namibia at the young age of 27. At 35, she became a member of the SWAPO Politburo, a type of unelected one-party Congress. In 2003, she was appointed Minister of Finance. She is a serious proponent of fiscal responsibility, and the hallmark of her tenure was to limit government spending which helped create Namibia's first financial surpluses in its history. [lxxxv] Viewed as less political and more technically proficient, Kuugongelwa has good relations with key Namibian politicians. Her ability to navigate difficult political streams was apparent by her young appointments. In 2015, President-elect Dr. Geingob picked her as a popular choice to be the first Namibian woman Prime Minister. [lxxxvi]

She is proud of Namibia's #16 ranking in the world for gender gap index (which ranks gender equity) and she highlights the fact that nearly 40% of government Ministers are women. [lxxxvii] [lxxxviii] Prime Minister Kuugongelwa noted these three items as her biggest concerns for her administration:

1. Climate change
2. Racial and gender inequality
3. Youth unemployment, unequal income and farm ownership by large multinational corporations. [lxxxix]

Her greatest goals for Namibia are much different from many Western countries and shows a perspective that is sensitive to the environment and those who are most vulnerable around her.

Graphic Design Credit: Adel Berakdar: Jenoco Publishing.

CATHERINE SAMBA PANZA
President Central African Republic 2014 – 2016

Catherine Samba-Panza's selflessness helped temporarily stop a civil war and led to a peaceful transition to an elected government.

"When I came into office, I knew that I was going to respect the rules and not run for President. I had a specific mission which I accomplished."

The former Mayor of Bangui, Samba-Panza was viewed as non-partisan politician in the middle of the civil war. Her appointment as the head of the transitional government was accepted by both sides in the conflict. She called for negotiations, held an election and stepped down after an election produced a new government. [xc]

72

xci

DR. JOYCE BANDA
First Woman President of Malawi 2012 - 2014

"Women's leadership is under attack."

Joyce Banda was Malawi's first female President. She had a history of working to protect human rights, children, women, and the disabled. She rose through the ranks as a Member of Parliament, a Cabinet Minister, Foreign Minister of Malawi and, finally, Vice President prior to being elevated to the highest office in the country.

She ascended to the Presidency when her predecessor died. Her transition to power almost did not take place. Members of the old cabinet opposed her and she stood firm to her duty in the Constitution. When the top general and former President supported her she was sworn in. Her victory in securing office was considered a triumph for democracy. During her time in office, she was declared the most powerful woman in Africa by Forbes magazine. [xcii]

[27] The President she had replaced had left Malawi's relations with the UN and traditional aid nations in tatters. She immediately set about repairing and restoring those relations, which left her open to the charge of being an absentee President. Her efforts paid off in international assistance. Her other primary accomplishment was the Prevention of Domestic Violence Bill which protected women and children in the home. She exercised prudent financial restraints and forced her Cabinet to resign when it was reported to be widely corrupt. She is also known for her work combatting hunger and establishing the African Federation of Women Entrepreneurs. [xciii] She was defeated in her bid to stay in office. She has subsequently worked in the Wilson Center in Washington, DC on increasing women in leadership and desires to return to Malawi, despite dangers to herself.

---

[27]   Source: Liberian Embassy

AMINATA 'MIMI' TOURE
Prime Minister of Senegal 2013 - 2014

"There is no place on the planet where you are having as much growth as Africa. You are seeing 6 – 12% growth."

Aminata 'Mimi' Toure was an active Communist and soccer player (football) in College for the Dakar Gazelles.[xciv] She was a known women's and human rights advocate throughout West Africa. She wrote her PhD Thesis on Micro-Financing of Women in Sub Sahara

---

[28] Photo Source: SeneNews

Africa. She headed the Gender, Human Rights and Culture Department at the United Nations Populations Fund. She stresses that smart health programs are based in gender equality. [xcv] As Minister of Justice for Senegal 2012 - 2013, she reduced corruption and was pro women's rights, human rights, and LGBT rights. As PM, she targeted corrupt officials.[xcvi] [xcvii] She was seen as efficient and incorruptible. Her term ended when she did not secure re-election.[xcviii]

Subsequently, she has worked throughout Africa as an Election Monitor for the Carter Center. Still a powerhouse in Senegal politics, she led a coalition of parties called United in Hope to a majority in the Federal elections, but she left the coalition when she suspected nepotism in the appointment of a rival as President of the Assembly.[29]

Soccer player to Prime Minister. Graphic: Dall-E open AI: Jenoco Pub.

---

[29]

https://en.wikipedia.org/wiki/Aminata_Tour%C3%A9_(Senegalese_politician)

LUISA DIOGO

1st Woman Prime Minister of Mozambique 2004 - 2010

"Working and struggling are things that do not scare us women."

Luisa Diogo began working in Mozambique's Finance Ministry while still in College (she later attended the London School of Economics). Newly independent Mozambique was destabilized from a civil war, which served as a proxy war between the U.S.S.R and the U.S. The country was devastated and it is believed that millions died. Diogo served in the Communist backed government and soon impressed the administration, rising to be

Director of the National Budget in 1989. After serving as Budget Director she worked at the World Bank in the Mozambique division. In 1994 she was appointed Deputy Finance Minister and then Finance Minister from 2004 - 2010. Poverty was the primary issue that Diogo addressed and she was uniquely qualified to find grants that Mozambique was eligible for. Under her tenure, almost 60% of the government's budget was comprised of grants and aids. [c] Diogo brought in nearly a billion dollars for agriculture, telecom, business development and the fight against AIDS. These funds were essential to preventing the Mozambique economy from collapsing. [ci]

In 2004, she was appointed Prime Minister during a vacancy in the office. She was seen as the standard bearer for a new generation. As Prime Minister, she:

- ➢ Expanded health care and an AIDS Emergency Program.
- ➢ Expanded education access
- ➢ Reformed the corrupt judicial system and police departments
- ➢ Combatted poverty with several programs, initiatives and grants. [cii]

ciii

HALIMAH JACOB
President of Singapore 2017 -2023

Jacob's father died when she was young and at an early age she would help her mother with her vending cart selling food near a bus station. As a young professional she worked in the National Trade Union Congress office as a legal assistant and in time became the Director of the Singapore Institute for Labor Studies. Elected to Parliament from her district she rose to lead Parliament from 3013 – 2017. She stood for and won the uncontested Presidential election of 2017, as the office was set aside for an ethnic Malay that term and she was deemed the most qualified.[31]

At first she remained in public housing, an unheard of practice for a national leader, true to her unassuming, humble persona. During the Covid crisis she focused on keeping the public safe and did something else that was quite remarkable. She used emergency provisions and tapped the national reserve surplus and increased the wages of workers across Singapore during the crisis, stabilizing an unsettling period of time. She is considered approachable and a leader of all Singaporeans.[32]

[31] https://simple.wikipedia.org/wiki/Halimah_Yacob
[32] https://www.abc.net.au/news/2023-09-20/singapore-president-halimah-yacob-female-muslim-end-term/102874778

SHEIKH HASINA
Prime Minister of Bangladesh
1996 – 2001, 2009 – Present

Sheikh Hasina grew up in one of Bangladesh's most influential political families. Her father, Sheikh Mujibar Rahman, was a founding father of the modern Bangladesh state and its first President. In 1975, he was overthrown by a military coup during which he, Hasina's mother and three of her siblings were assassinated.

Only Hasina and her sister survived because they were out of the country at the time. When home in Bangladesh in 1981, election fraud and oppression were commonplace and she dedicated herself and made the country more stable, democratic and less violent. [cv]

She was elected to lead the 'Awami League Party,' but was soon arrested and spent time under house arrest. Even under house arrest, she remained so powerful that in 1990 General Ershad, a coup leader, stepped down at her insistence and the presence of massive protests. [cvi] In the early 1990s, Hasina headed the opposition to Khaleda Zia's government, another iconic Bangladeshi woman leader. Hasina and her party kept insisting on a neutral caretaker government to take office before the next election to ensure the fairness of the results. Zia's government refused at first, but then gave in after a boycott of an election.

With a neutral government in place, Hasina won election as Prime Minister. Young Hasina with her father. [cvii] [cviii]   In 1996, she was sworn in as the second female Prime Minister of Bangladesh. Despite laws passed and her great effort, political and social turmoil continued in Bangladesh throughout the 1990s and 2000s. When she lost re-election in 2001, she stepped down in a peaceful transition and led the opposition for seven years.

In 2004, she was targeted in an assassination attempt that killed 24 people and injured more than 300. She experienced loss of hearing in one ear as a result. In 2007, she was arrested for extortion but was exonerated and released in time to stand for election in 2009. All three of her terms, have been marred by violence and instability[cix] Her administrations accomplished the following:

> Passed election reform in 1996.
> Negotiated the groundbreaking 'Chittagong Hill Tracts Peace Accord' in 1997.
> Banned the use of landmines and awarded the 'Mother Teresa Award,' and the 'Gandhi Award' for promoting peace and democracy. [cx]

cxi

AUNG SANG SUU KYI
State Counselor/Foreign Minister Myanmar 2016 – 2021.

"The only real prison is fear, and the only real freedom is freedom from fear."

Aung San Suu Kyi was born to a political family in Burma at the end of the Second World War. Her father, Aung San, was the Prime Minister of colonial Burma from 1946 – 1947 and is considered the Founding Father of Burma. He was assassinated just months before Burma's independence, for which he had fought as a guerrilla. Aung San Suu Kyi's mother served as   Ambassador to the United States in the 1960s.

She attended school and University in India and Great Britain, married and spent more than twenty years living in Britain and raising a family. She returned to Burma in 1988 to care for her mother when she fell ill. When she arrived, the military dictatorship that ruled Burma, now called Myanmar, was ruthlessly massacring protesters. She publicly spoke out against the repression attracting the attention of the dictatorship. She was arrested and held incommunicado. While in prison, she was offered her freedom if she left the country. She refused and chose prison until all political prisoners were free and fair elections could be held.[cxii] Two years later in 1990, Myanmar held its first democratic election in decades. Aung San Suu Kyi's party won in a landslide. But the junta ignored the results and continued to imprison her. She was awarded the Nobel Prize for Peace in 1991. [cxiii]

Once free, Suu Kyi founded an assembly which was independent of the Junta; she was immediately re-arrested and held for two years. In 2003, the newly released Aung was placed under house arrest when protestors clashed with authorities. This time the term of her sentence was to be renewed yearly. [cxiv] While under house arrest, a fan swam the moat to visit her. The Junta used this as an excuse to extend her prison sentence to miss the election. She was prohibited from standing for election by a new law that prohibited convicted criminals from standing for office. Her party (NLD) disbanded in protest and did not participate in the 2010 election.[cxv]

In 2011, her party was re-registered and she gained control of it in a difficult inter-party campaign. The junta once again held elections in 2015. This time there was no boycott and her party, the NLD won a large majority. Because she was still officially restricted from holding office, Aung San Suu Kyi made her political advisor Prime Minister. [cxvi] Today, Aung San Suu Kyi now holds power behind the scenes as the State Counsellor and is, effectively, the Prime Minister.

Assuming office in 2016 as State Counsellor and then Foreign Minister was added to her portfolio, hopes were high that Myanmar would finally change its abysmal human rights record towards its minorities. At first when she came into office she started off on the right foot, granting amnesty to student protestors who had been arrested and forming a commission to study the treatment of the Rohingya minority in one of the states. Unfortunately, the violence against the Rohingya and other minorities, the Shen, and the Karen, continued at the hands of the military she was now ostensibly in charge of, or at least now associated with. She did not speak out against the genocide against the Rohingya and spoke harshly about journalists who had been arrested covering the Rohingya story. Public opinion about her turned abruptly around the world and numerous human rights awards and honorary citizenships were revoked from her as a result of her complicity or perceived indifference.[33] No one knows what behind-the-scenes dynamics were happening during her term. But her actions puzzled and conflicted generations of supporters. Was she trying to ingratiate herself and prove her trustworthiness to the military regime to stay in charge so behind the scenes she could lessen the destructive human rights policies? Was she biding her time until she was stronger and could exercise better control of the dangerous military structure that was impervious to criticism or revolt? Or did she change? Had years in prison and under house arrest weaken her resolve to counter her former foe the military and its implacable power? Or did she just look the other way and allow the abuse to continue unabated and enjoy the relative safety and prestige of her position? No one can say for sure but Suu Kyi, however, not surprisingly, in 2021 the military junta overthrew her and her government, jailed her and charged her with charges ranging from corruption to violations of Official Secrets Act to a garden variety of minor charges. She was sentenced to 27 years in prison and has been in jail in frail health since 2021. The tragedy of Aung San Suu Kyi is Shakespearian in nature as so many of these women leaders are deposed. She was finally given a chance to reform the beast that had persecuted her for her whole life and was implicated by her association with it and her inability or unwillingness to reform it. So the world turned against her, and the beast - the military junta, swallowed her whole, again.

---

[33] https://en.wikipedia.org/wiki/Aung_San_Suu_Kyi

cxvii

BIDHYA BHANDARI

1st Woman Elected President of Nepal
2015 – 2023.

*"My election is the first step toward assuring the new
constitutional guarantees of equality for women."*

Nepal was a monarchy until recently, so Bhandari's work for the Communist Party had taken place under-ground. She rose up the ranks of the Party and married an aspiring politician and guerilla leader. In 1993, her husband Madan Bhandari was killed in a suspicious car crash. She returned to politics and was was elected to Parliament, defeating a former Prime Minister to replace her husband. She was re-elected in 1994 and 1999 and served as the Minister of Environment and Population during the 1990s. [cxviii] In 2006, she was part of the leadership of the revolution that forced the

Monarchy to accept democracy. [cxix]
Photo: Bidhya with her husband Madan in their youth.

From 2009 to 2011, she was appointed Minister of Defense for Nepal and was instrumental in encouraging the Maoist guerillas to peacefully disarm and integrate into society. In 2015, she became President and successfully pushed the Constitutional Convention to include a 30% quota for women-only seats in Parliament.[cxx]

cxxi

TSAI ING-WEN
1st Woman Elected President of Taiwan 2016 – Present

"I will never be able to forgive myself if I choose not to do what I know I can."

When Tsai was a student her parents were disappointed that she did not score first in all her examinations like her older siblings. She wanted to study archaeology but pursued a law degree as her father desired. The Cornell and London School of Economics graduate and policy wonk was picked by President Lee Teng-hui to formulate a "two-state" theory to show that Taiwan and China are legally separate states. [cxxii] The government of Taiwan is the result of the Chinese Civil War when the Republic forces were defeated by the Communist rebels and allowed to retreat to Taiwan.

Tsai became the head of the Mainland Affairs Council, a Cabinet-level agency responsible for China policy. She joined the DPP in 2004 and was briefly Vice-Premier under former President Chen Shui-bian. [cxxiii] In 2012, she made her first run for President and garnered 46% of the vote in a close contest. She was strengthened by the Sunflower Student Movement, an anti-mainland-China-influence movement. Tsai lng-wen ran for President in 2016 and won, beating her closest opponent by 25% points. [cxxiv]

Tsai and her party are proponents of Taiwan's independence and draw a clear distinction from the mainland Chinese government. She treads carefully, however, not to provoke China. She is a proponent of LGBT rights, youth, women and the poor. [cxxv]

She remains single and dotes on her cats.

PARK GEUN-HYE
President of South Korea 2013 – 2016

"How is Daejeon?"

Park Guen-hye, after waking from an assassination attempt,
worried about the people in the City, not the attempt on her life.

90

Park Geun-hye's life reads like a Shakespearian play. Born to a powerful ruling family, in which both of her parents were assassinated. She was comforted in her loneliness by a friend whose future actions would betray and doom her own political career just when she reached the apogee of South Korean power.

She grew up as the daughter of South Korea's third President and dictator Park Chung-hee. She lived in the 'Blue House,' the South Korean equivalent to the 'White House.' Her father's eighteen-year rule was economically very successful; it was also controversial and brutal. Human rights were not respected and Park Chung-hee persecuted the opposition ruthlessly. This led to several assassination attempts on his life. One attempt left Park Geun-hye without her mother. Her mother was assassinated by accident instead of her father in 1974. So, at the age of 22, Park Geun-Hye was called upon to serve in place of her mother as the de facto First Lady of South Korea. She was charged with receiving the spouses of foreign heads of state at the Blue House.[cxxvii] After her father's assassination by his head of security, Park Geun-hye fled.

When Park's father was assassinated, she became close to Choi Soon-sil, the daughter of an influential but controversial religious Minister. The friendship helped Park with her loneliness and violent loss of both her mother and father. This is the same woman whose controversy would bring down Park's Presidency.

For the next nearly twenty years Park was a prolific author, writing and publishing several books including: *If I were Born in an Ordinary Family*, 1993, *In the End, Only a Speck*, 1998, *Befriending Adversity, My Mother Yul Young-soo*, 1999, *Journey of My Mind*, 1999. [cxxviii] For many years after her father's assassination she lived a private life.

In the mid to late 1990s, Park emerged and was elected to serve as the Vice Chairman of the 'Grand National Party' for the next six years and was subsequently elected five terms to the Korean National Assembly. [cxxix] In 2006 the curse of her family returned. She survived an assassination attempt which left her with a scar on her face. When she regained consciousness after surgery, her first words were: "How is Daejeon?" She voiced concern for the city where the attempt took place rather than her own condition. [cxxx]

In her preparation to run for the Presidency of South Korea, she issued a humble public apology for the human rights violations which occurred during her father's dictatorship. [cxxxi] In 2012, her Party nominated Park as their candidate for the Presidential election. In poignant irony, her opponent was a human rights lawyer who had been imprisoned by her father. Park won the Presidency with the campaign slogan "Let's live well," harkening back to the good economic times of her father's regime. [cxxxii] As President, Park identified four evils she wished to rid from South Korea: domestic violence, sexual violence, school violence and unsafe food. She was named the most powerful woman in Asia by Forbes magazine in 2013 and 2014, and by other publications as early as 1999.

Her term was hobbled by a weak economy which was not helped by the Samsung Galaxy 7 phone controversy. They were produced in South Korea and known to burst into flames. Her administration ended with a scandal that reduced her favorable rating to five percent - the lowest in South Korean history. [cxxxiii] [cxxxiv]

She was impeached, removed from office in December of 2016 and is in jail awaiting her trial. Her supposed crime was to give her friend, Choi Soon-sil, influence in her administration. Choi is accused of making phone calls on her own daughter's behalf to help her gain entry in college; she is also accused of editing some of Geun-hye's speeches and steering campaign donors to Geun-hye's favorite charities. Park Geun-hye is facing more than 10 years in prison if she is not exonerated.[cxxxv] Park is single and is a very private person who prefers to dine alone. She is now prisoner 503.

Graphic Image: Adel Berakdar: Jenoco Publications.

YINGLUCK SHINAWATRA
1st Female Prime Minister of Thailand, 2011 – 2014.

"Females are symbols of nonviolence... a female is more compromising. A female can talk with anyone easily."

Yingluck is the younger sister of Thaksin Shinawatra, the wealthy businessman turned Prime Minister of Thailand from 2001 – 2006. [cxxxvi] He was overthrown by a military coup and is prevented from running for office again. In his absence, Yingluck became the Director of two of his companies, a telecommunications giant and a large property management company.

Educated at Kentucky State University in the United States, Shinawatra had never run for public office when she threw her hat in the ring during the 2011 election for Prime Minister. She won in a landslide, being perceived as a legitimate extension of her brother's mandate and a breath of fresh air from outside the political world.

After her election, she said:

"I plan to work hard. People will trust me, as long as the government preserves the rule of law and treats people fairly. As long as we solve problems, I hope (the) Thai people will give me a chance to prove myself and show my sincerity." [cxxxvii]

Early in her term, severe flooding hit the capital of Bangkok and much of the country, crippling her early momentum. Her term was cut short by a controversial Constitutional Court verdict which found her guilty of 'abuse of power' for transferring a civil servant to a different department with a hidden agenda. She was arrested, her government was dissolved and she was barred from political activity for five years.

Her accomplishments during her term included:

> ➤ A five-billion-dollar flood recovery fund.
> ➤ Created a compensation fund for families of deceased, unfairly injured or detained citizens.

➢ Sponsored a political amnesty Bill to foster an era of reconciliation (this proved to be controversial and set off large protests, in part it was seen as an effort to allow her brother to return). [cxxxviii]

She kept a low profile after her release from jail for a couple of years but recently has begun appearing in public again to great fanfare. While not technically campaigning, Yingluck held Facebook contests to figure where she will visit. She has been met with rapturous crowds and has remained very popular. [cxxxix] She is currently fighting the corruption charges in court that the dictatorship has brought. The case and her plight does not seem likely to end soon.

cxl

ROZA OTUNBAYEVA
1st Woman President of Kyrgyzstan
2010 – 2011.

"I am a fighter. I believe in a bright future for my country. I believe that the people of my country deserve a decent life, and I know that my people want to live in freedom." [cxli]

Roza Otunbayeva served on the Faculty of the Philosophy Department at Kyrgyz State University after her graduation from College. At the time, Kyrgyz was an S.S.R in the Soviet Union and not independent. Roza began her political career working as an Undersecretary of the Communist Party in Kyrgyzstan. She was elevated to Soviet Ambassador to Malaysia and became Ambassador to the United States of the newly independent state and then its Foreign Minister. [cxlii] In 2004, Roza formed her own political party because of a split with President Akayev, accusing him of corruption.

A popular uprising known as the "Tulip Revolution" was backed by Roza and removed President Akayev from office peacefully.

Otunbayeva was appointed Foreign Minister in the next administration but the majority of the Parliament rejected her nomination. [cxliii] Not to be put off, Roza campaigned and won a seat in the National Parliament and rose to lead the opposition to the new Bakiyev Presidency. She believed him to be corrupt as well. Soon a violent uprising overthrew Bakiyev. Roza was left as one of the most powerful leaders in the nation and was asked to form an Interim government until elections could be held. When elections were held in 2011, Roza stepped down in Kyrgyzstan's first peaceful transfer of power, perhaps her greatest accomplishment. [cxliv]

cxlv

GLORIA MACAPAGAL-ARROYO
President of the Philippines
2001 – 2010.

"Optimism is infectious, and opportunity irresistible. Progress follows progress. Someone, even government, just has to get it started." cxlvi

Gloria Macapagal Arroyo grew up in one of the most powerful households in the Philippines. Her father was President Macapagal who served a popular term in the early 1960s. She was a Professor of Economics in her early professional career. Her introduction to government was her 1987 appointment as Assistant Secretary for Trade and industry in President Corazon 'Cory' Aquino's Administration (the first female President of the Philippines). She served in the Philippine Senate during the 1990s and was elected Vice President to President Estrada in 1998. It was an unusual situation because she was from an opposition party. [cxlvii]When he was accused of corruption, she retained the Vice Presidency and resigned from his Cabinet. This proved to be a wise move because when he was ousted, she became President by succession.

She served out his term and was elected to a six-year term of her own. Her election in 2004 was controversial because there were significant voting irregularities. So much so, that when she stepped down in 2010, she was arrested on election fraud charges in 2011. Later, she was arrested on charges of stealing from the national lottery. She spent four years in prison from 2012 – 2016, where her health deteriorated rapidly. In 2016 the Supreme Court found her not guilty of all charges and she was released from prison, an interviewer remarked that she looked much better than when she was in prison, she responded.

"Freedom agrees with me."

cxlviii

KHALEDA ZIA
1st Woman Prime Minister of Bangladesh
1991–1996, 2001–2006.

"It is impossible to practice parliamentary politics without having patience, decency, politeness and courtesy."

Khaleda Zia was the first female Prime Minister of Bangladesh serving two terms in 1991–96 and 2001–06. She presided over a period of unrest and natural disasters.

Her husband was a leader of the independence movement for Bangladesh, its first Interim Prime Minister and its 7th Prime Minister taking office in 1977. Upon his assassination in 1981, she became politically active, and in a few years, became the leader of his political party, the BNP. Zia was arrested repeatedly during the dictatorship in the 1980s. Once she was free, she worked hard to build her party and, in 1991, won the election to become the first female Prime Minister of Bangladesh. [cxlix] Photo: Wikipedia.

Her primary efforts and accomplishments of her first term include:

➤ Improved schools.
➤ Improved economic opportunities for women.

She won re-election in a landslide, but most of the opposition boycotted the election. After massive protests about election fraud, she stepped down for the stability of the country. In the next election, she won handily and served a second term. At the end of her term, the military stepped in again and arrested her on corruption charges. The arrest was a humiliating affair as she was dragged out of her house in the middle of the night in her nightgown in front of T.V cameras. She and Bangladesh's only other female Prime Minister, Sheikh Hasina, have been deadlocked in a political competition that verges on violence among their supporters. Recently, an arrest warrant has been issued for Zia due to her celebrating her birthday on a controversial day. [cl][cli] She has also charged her with arson as of the writing of this edition.

34

CHANDIKA BANDARANAIKE KUMARATUNGA
1st Woman President of Sri Lanka 1994 – 2005
Prime Minister of Sri Lanka 1994.

"Reconciliation is impossible without accepting the mistakes of the past." [clii]

Chandrika Kumaratunga is the daughter of the world's first elected female Prime Minister Sirimavo Bandaranaike. She is also the daughter of the 4th Prime Minister of Sri Lanka Solomon Bandaranaike. Kumaratunga grew up in the most powerful political household in her nation. In her youth, while a student in Paris, she took a leadership role in the anarchist/student/communist revolution of 1968 which toppled the French Fourth Republic government. It is

---

[34] Photo: Simple English Wikipedia

ironic because in 1971 a similar student revolution almost toppled the democratic rule of her mother. Returning to Ceylon (Sri Lanka's colonial name), When her husband was assassinated, she left the country for a self-imposed exile to Great Britain, working at the UN University. [cliii] When she returned to Sri Lanka in 1993, she won election as Minister of the Western Province, and in 1994 she became Prime Minister of Sri Lanka. In the following Presidential election, she prevailed and became the first woman to serve as President of Sri Lanka, a now more powerful position that Prime Minister. She then appointed her mother Prime Minister. She and her mother had been at times both allies and competitors in recent years. The characteristics of her terms were:

- ➤ She appointed her mother Prime Minister
- ➤ She tried to make peace with the Tamil separatists, then when that failed, renewed the war with vigor.
- ➤ She was blinded in one eye in an assassination attempt. [cliv]

She won re-election for a second term which was plagued by internecine fighting within her cabinet over the proposed peace terms with the Tamil insurgency. Toward the end of her term she assumed direct control over most of the powerful ministries herself, opening herself up to the charge of becoming a dictator. [clv]

MEGAWATI SUKARNOPUTRI
1st Woman President of Indonesia
2001 – 2004.

"I want to encourage our people to have the courage to understand and fight for their rights."

Megawati Sukarnoputri was the daughter of President Sukarno, the first President of an independent Indonesia. Her father was forced out by General Suharto after a confusing series of events when the Communist Party assassinated all of the country's top general except for General Suharto who oversaw the Reserves. Megawati's father,

---

35 Photo: Wikipedia.

President Sukarno, was found in the custody of the Communists at the airport, however, it is unknown whether he was being held against his will or was a co-conspirator. Suharto, the surviving general, rose to power as dictator, eclipsed Sukarno's (Megawati's father) rule. It is no wonder that Megawati walked a careful path with the military in her ascendency to the Presidency forty years later.

Megawati went to College but never graduated. She was elected to the National Assembly in the late 1980s and rose quickly to become the Director of the Indonesian Democratic Party (IDP). She was viewed by many as a viable alternative to the dictator Suharto (who had replaced her father). Suharto had her removed as head of the IDP so she couldn't challenge him in the next election. This led to widespread unrest and she was further restricted from running for *any* office in the upcoming elections. When Suharto stepped down in 1998 for health reasons, it was widely expected that Megawati would replace him, but the male dominated National Assembly chose Habibi and Wahid, each for brief terms. [clvi]

The outcry for passing over Megawati was massive and she was soon offered the Vice Presidency and then was handed over most of the functions of the day to day government, as the blind and ill President Wahid was unable to undertake most of his executive duties. In 2001, she was finally voted into the Presidency by the National Assembly.

In late 2001, Laskar Jihad, a radical Muslim militia founded to avenge Christian massacres of Muslims in the Moluccas Islands, had vowed to kill all the Christians in Sulawesi by Christmas. On December 2nd they began the forewarned massacre in the towns of Tentena and Poso. Megawati quickly sent 4,000 Indonesian troops to stop the massacre, the first such action ever undertaken by the Indonesia government. [clvii] Later, Jafar Umar Thalib, the head of Laskar Jihad, was arrested and the group disbanded. This quick and decisive human rights action saved tens of thousands of lives but received little media attention.

As a child with her father, Indira Gandhi and Nehru: in her teens with her father Sukarno.

This was also the time of a massive terrorist attack on Bali which killed more than 300 people, and an attack on the Indonesian Parliament was targeted by Aceh separatists. Megawati would fail to win re-election and also failed in a comeback attempt. Her four years at the helm of Indonesia could easily have ended in greater bloodshed had it not been for her steady and quiet leadership. [clviii]

Members of Laskar Jihad with machetes in 2001.

TANSU CILLER
1st Female Prime Minister of Turkey, 1993 – 1996.

Ciller was born into wealth, and she and her husband earned more than $50 million in real estate. She was elected to Parliament in 1991 and appointed Economic Minister that year. The economic downturn during her term hurt her pledge for a balanced budget. [clix] Her term as PM was plagued by fighting with Kurdish separatists and economic strife and she lost re-election. She was re-elected to head her party, but resigned when her party was defeated in 2002. [clx]

BENAZIR BHUTTO
1st Muslim Woman Prime Minister in The World
1st Woman Prime Minister of Pakistan
1988 – 1990, 1993 – 1996.

At the age of 35, Benazir Bhutto became the youngest Prime Minister in the world and the first Muslim female Prime Minister. Bhutto is the daughter of Zulfikar Bhutto the ninth Prime Minister of Pakistan who was deposed by General Zia who became dictator of Pakistan. Bhutto's father was put on trial and sentenced to death. Just before his execution his last words were: "Oh Lord, help me for... I am innocent." [clxii] After the coup, the Oxford and Harvard-educated Benazir Bhutto continued her father's legacy by heading his political party the Pakistan People's Party. She fought to restore democracy and human rights throughout Pakistan. For this she was imprisoned and finally exiled from Pakistan.

She continued to lead the opposition from exile with the hope of one day returning and leading Pakistan back to democracy. She returned from exile to Pakistan in 1986. When General Zia-al-Haq died in a plane crash in 1988, Bhutto won the subsequent election and became Prime Minister. She had given birth only three months before assuming office! In less than two years, her government was unconstitutionally dismissed. Undeterred, she led the opposition in the National Assembly for three years until she was reelected on October 16, 1993. [clxiii] Her accomplishments during her two terms in office were significant:

> ➢ Built 24,000 schools in three years.
> ➢ Electricity was brought to almost all villages across Pakistan.
> ➢ Benazir Bhutto worked closely with the United States on anti-terrorism and the war on drugs. [clxiv]

In 1995, her second government was also dismissed. She went into exile in Britain where she continued to lead her party. Bhutto was convicted of corruption, in absentia, and sentenced to three years in prison. Bhutto returned to Pakistan in October 2007, when the Dictator Musharraf granted her amnesty and alluded to the possibility of a power-sharing agreement if she returned. [clxv] At her homecoming

109

rally a suicide bomber killed more than 136 people, narrowly missing her. The Dictator Musharraf instituted Martial Law and arrested her.[clxvi] After her release, she was assassinated by bomb on December 27th, 2007, at a rally.[clxvii] She was so mourned, that her widow, Asif Zardari, was elected PM from 2008 – 2013.

CORAZON 'CORY' AQUINO
1st Woman President in Asia and the Philippines
1986 – 1992 clxviii clxix

*"I would rather die a meaningful death than
to live a meaningless life."*

Corazon Aquino was the first female President of the Philippines.[clxx] She was named TIME 'Woman of the Year' in 1986 when she led the People Power (or Yellow) Revolution which restored democracy to her country.

In her youth, she spent several years in the U.S during the late 1940s – early 1950s and attended Mount St Vincent College in New York. She met her husband in law school, though neither finished school. Despite her waning interest in politics, she supported her husband's successful run for the Senate of the Philippines. Her husband, Senator Benigno Aquino (nicknamed Ninoy), was a bitter critic of the Marcos dictatorship and was imprisoned for eight years. Upon his release, he went into exile in the United States. In 1983, he was allowed to return to the Philippines and was assassinated at his homecoming. [clxxi]

After her husband's assassination, "Cory" took up the leadership position of the opposition. The dictator Marcos sought an election to legitimize his regime to the world and Cory was drafted as a reluctant opposition candidate. Marcos highlighted her inexperience and attacked her with sexist remarks, she responded: that she had "no experience in cheating, lying to the public, stealing government money, and killing political opponents." [clxxii]   Marcos was declared the winner of the election, but there was widespread election fraud. As a result Aquino led a peaceful revolution against the Marcos regime (the "Yellow" revolution because of their yellow ribbons or the "People's Power" revolution) encouraging civil disobedience, mass strikes and boycotts. It worked. Her revolution was enthusiastically supported and even when Marcos sent the troops out to break up the protests, the protests grew in size. Ultimately Marcos fled the country, conceded the election and Cory Aquino became the first female President of the Philippines. Subsequently, the military officers responsible for her husband's death were put on trial and found guilty. At the end of her term, she steadfastly refused to run for re-election.

Among her greatest achievements as President were, she:

➤ Called a Constitutional Commission to help draft a new, more democratic, Constitution.
➤ She empowered a commission to retain the stolen wealth Marcos had taken from the Philippines.
➤ Human and civil rights were respected and protected.
➤ Held peace talks with communist and Muslim insurgents.
➤ Paid off billions of dollars of debt, stabilizing the economy.
➤ In 1992, she refused to run for another term, setting a good democratic precedent. [clxxiii] [clxxiv]

GOLDA MEIR
1st Woman Prime Minister of Israel, 1969 – 1974.^{clxxv}

"It's no accident many accuse me of conducting public affairs with my heart instead of my head. Well, what if I do? Those who don't know how to weep with their whole heart don't know how to laugh either."^{clxxvi}

"Not being beautiful was the true blessing. Not being beautiful forced me to develop my inner resources. The pretty girl has a handicap to overcome."

---

[37] Photo: Wikimedia Commons.

Golda Meir was born in Ukraine and immigrated to Milwaukie, Wisconsin, United States as a young girl. At 23, she immigrated to British Palestine (the future site of Israel) with her husband. In 1924, she became an official of a powerful Trade Union and a manager in a construction company.

At the end of World War Two, the Israeli independence movement was gaining momentum against British rule when most of the male Jewish leadership was arrested. Meir was not arrested and became the head of the Jewish Agency's Political Department. [clxxvii]

She was an effective and successful international spokesperson for the Independence of Israel. In 1948, she served as Israel's First Ambassador to the Soviet Union, and soon after, was elected to the Israeli Parliament, the Knesset. In the 1950s she held Ministerial positions for Labor and Foreign Minister from 1956 – 1966. During her term, as Foreign Secretary, she built relations around the world. [clxxviii]

When Prime Minister Eshkol died in office, Meir was voted in as Prime Minister by her party, becoming the first woman in the Middle East elected Head of State. She was also the first female Israeli Prime Minster and only the third woman in the world to be elected to lead a nation (after Sirimavo Bandaranaike of Sri Lanka and Indira Gandhi of India). [clxxix] [clxxx]

As Prime Minister, her generals misjudged the neighboring Arab nations' intentions as they prepared to invade Israel in 1973, on Yom Kippur, a Jewish religious holiday. In the first days of the Yom Kippur War, Israel did not fare well. Unlike the Six-Day War, where Israel had, only a few years earlier, devastated its neighbors' Air Forces and won the land war within days. But the Yom Kippur War

Golda laughing:[clxxxi]

saw Israel's resources stretched thin. The Arab neighbors pushed Israeli forces deep into their territory. At a crucial point she realized that Egypt's Sadat was about to make a strategic blunder. "People know when they have lost. Some people don't know when they have won. Sadat doesn't know he's won."[38] She was right. If he kept his tanks safely entrench on the East of the Sinai, victory was his. But by pursuing the weakened Jewish position fresh from his victory, he exposed his tanks to massacre as well as trapping his entire 3rd Army in starvation conditions. The Israeli armed forces pushed the Syrian forces out of Israel into their own territories. Sadat famously recognized her as Prime Minister of Israel, a precondition to negotiate a truce, the first Arab nation to do so. The peace talks led to the 1978 Camp David Accord between Israel and Egypt. Meir was widely blamed for the near defeat and heavy casualties, tired battling cancer, she retired from office. [clxxxii]

---

[38] Golda, the 2023 film.

SOONG QINGLING
1st Woman Vice-President of China
1968 – 1974.

"Women of the East and West, unite to change the world! Unite to demand universal disarmament and the abolition of policies of discrimination and unequal treaties and we women will certainly be successful."[clxxxiii]

---

[39] Photo: Wikimedia Commons.

Soong Qingling is a rare person who has served at the highest levels of leadership in both Republican China and Communist China. She was married to Sun Yat Sen, the academic revolutionary who was the Republic of China's first President. She migrated across the political spectrum from being Madame Sun Yat Sen to become a top leader of the Chinese Communist Party and elevated to the highest position a woman has ever held in Communist China to date, in her own right.

Qingling with Sun Yat Sen, her husband, with Chiang Kai Shek and her sister, Madame Chiang Kai Shek. Photo Source: G.W.U

Educated in Wellesley College in Georgia, United States, she returned to mainland China while it was a democratic republic struggling against dictatorial tendencies and powerful warlords. Her husband, Sun Yat Sen, had been the moving force behind China's creation of a democracy after the overthrow of the Ching Dynasty. He served as the founding President over a fractured China, where war lords, dynastic pretenders, external threats and the early rise of communist rebels presented overwhelming stresses on the new republic.

Soong was one of three famous Qingling sisters. Her younger sister, Mai-ling, married General Chiang Kai Shek, who would follow Sun Yat Sen as leader of Republican China. When Sun Yat Sen died in 1925 of cancer, Soong Qingling became part of the communist leadership. Her brother-in-law, Chiang Kai Shek, known as the

The three Qingling Sisters.

Generalissimo, now led the fledgling Republic with Mai-ling at his side. When the Republican government expelled the communists from the government, Soong resigned and went to Moscow and Shanghai for most of the next twenty years.

During this time, a long brutal civil war broke out between the Republic of China and the communist rebels. When Japan invaded China, the Republic and communists temporarily put their differences aside and united to fight the Japanese. After the defeat of the Japanese by the allies, the Civil [40]War reignited between Mao's communists and the

---

[40] Wikimedia.

Republic of China. The new civil war took a surprising turn with Shek losing territory to the growing communist insurgency. Ultimately, Shek's Republican government lost the war and was allowed to retreat to Taipei (Taiwan) and establish itself there.

Soong had been raising money for the communists since the late 1930s. When the Communist rebels were victorious, she was given a special place in the new regime. Over time, Soong's role and visibility increased. She was present in several high-profile delegations to visit heads of states around the world. She held several shared Vice Presidential positions within the party and government and served as the joint Vice-President of China from 1959 – 1975. She is credited with having served as 'acting President' from 1968 – 1972; but there is little evidence to support this claim. [clxxxiv clxxxv clxxxvi] She was often criticized during the 'Cultural Revolution,' but was given 'protected status' by Mao and Chou Enlai and was left undisturbed.

Soong standing near Mao Tse Tung.

Soong's accomplishments in the People's Republic of China:

- ➢ Served as Vice President
- ➢ Led the Chinese Welfare Institution
- ➢ Chaired the All-China Women's Federation
- ➢ Founded the magazine *China Rebuilds* (*China Today*)[clxxxvii]

120

clxxxviii INDIRA GANDHI
1st Woman Prime Minister of India
2nd Woman Elected Head of State in the World
1966 – 1977, 1980 – 1984.

Indira Gandhi attended Swiss boarding schools as a child and Oxford University for College. Her father was Nehru, the first Prime Minister of India as an independent nation. Indira Gandhi took her name from her husband, Feroze Gandhi, who is no relation to Mahatmas Gandhi. Before her father became Prime Minister he spent years in prison when she was a child. Photo: Wikimedia Commons

When her mother died of Tuberculosis when Indira was 19 years old, clxxxix she served as a sort of First Lady for her father during his terms as Prime Minister. This gave her incredible exposure to the most powerful people in the world and experience running the world's largest democracy. cxcIn 1955, she headed the Committee of the

Congress Party, establishing her credentials as a leader in her own right. When her father died of natural causes in 1964, she was elevated to Minister of Information, raising her profile across the nation. In 1966, when the new Prime Minister Shastri died suddenly, she was elected Prime Minister by her party. [cxci]

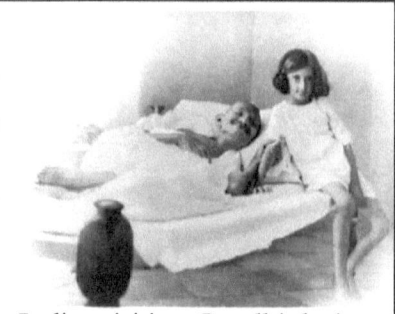

Indira visiting Gandhi during his hunger strike.

As India's first Woman Prime Minister and only the second elected female head of state in the world (see Sirimavo Bandaranaike, Sri Lanka), she worked to make India self-sufficient for its food supply. This was known as the 'Green Revolution.' [cxcii] One of her other greatest accomplishment, was both military and humanitarian in nature. In 1971, she sent Indian troops into Bangladesh while the Pakistani army massacred, raped and pillaged the Bangladeshi provinces to prevent Bangladesh from breaking away from it union with Pakistan. More than 3 million people were massacred by the Pakistani troops during this genocide, and hundreds of thousands of women were raped. Indira Gandhi sent in Indian troops to halt the bloodshed in an act of humanitarian rescue. Bangladesh received its independence after the removal of Pakistani forces. [cxciii cxciv]

"Forgiveness is a virtue of the brave."

After two reasonably successful terms, she began to show increasingly authoritarian tendencies in her bid to hang on to power. After a court found her guilty of corruption, she stayed in power for a third term by declaring Martial Law and suspending the Constitution. This is sometimes known as the 'reign of terror.' She also championed a controversial sterilization policy of men to curb population growth. Remarkably, after a term out of office, she was elected to an unprecedented fourth term in 1980. In 1984, Gandhi was assassinated by her own Sikh bodyguards after deadly violence at a holy Sikh temple. [cxcv] Her son Rajiv also became Prime Minister. He too was tragically assassinated two years after he left office. [cxcvi]

cxcvii SIRIMAVO BANDARANAIKE
st Elected Woman Head of State in the World
1st Elected Woman in Asia and in Sri Lanka
1960 – 1965, 1970 – 1977, 1994 – 2000.

Bandaranaike served as the world's first female head of state. Her three separate terms spanned from the 1960s to the early 2000s, 1960 – 65, 1970 – 77, and 1994 – 2000.

Bandaranaike in her first term and in her last term. Photos: Wikimedia Commons.

Her accomplishments are groundbreaking and her family is also considered the most influential in Sri Lanka's history. Her father served in the Ceylon Senate (Sri Lanka's early/colonial name). Her husband, Solomon Bandaranaike, was the 4th Prime Minister of Ceylon from 1956 – 1959, and a founder of the United National Party. Her children also fared well in politics as Chandrika Kumaratunga served as President and Anura Bandaranaike was a Minister in several cabinets in his own right.

Her husband's assassination by a Buddhist monk in 1959 send the country into a tailspin. The interim government of his party's leadership proved weak and Sirimavo was asked to step into the power vacuum. She campaigned for Prime Minister on the promises to continue her husband's leftist economic policies and the removal of Tamils, an ethnic minority which was seeking independence, from Sri Lanka to the Indian mainland. [cxcviii]

Key characteristics of her first term were:

- She nationalized banking, insurance, and schools.
- Dropped English as the official language.
- Increased policies of deportation and discrimination against the Tamil minority.
- Became closer with the U.S.S.R and China while officially holding a policy of non-alignment. [cxcix]

During her second term, her government was almost overthrown by a student led revolution in 1971. The insurgents surrounded the Capital and her government had to be rescued by Indian and Pakistani troops. It was similar to the student led insurgency that toppled the government of France in 1968. She stood down the protests bravely. The major characteristics of her second term were:

- Put down a massive student led uprising.
- Introduced and ratified a new governing Constitution.
- Renamed Ceylon Sri Lanka.
- Closed and censored newspapers across the island.
- Delayed the election to buy time to regain her popularity. [cc]

None of these activities helped her re-election and she and her party were soundly defeated in 1977. Because of her delaying the elections, she was charged with abuse of power, removed from Parliament and banned from participating in politics for seven years. She spent the next nearly two decades as the leader of the opposition, often fighting off challenges to her power. She even had competition within her own family. In 1994 her daughter, Chandrika, became the next Prime Minister and then President. Bandaranaike became Prime Minister one last time, but the position was ceremonial and subordinate to her daughter, the President. Sadly, she died on Election Day 2000. [cci]

Five Decades *of* Women in Leadership

Women as Presidents or Prime Ministers have gone from rare to commonplace in most of the world in the past three decades.

The notable countries which are exceptions to this trend include the United States, China, Russia, Mexico, Japan, South Africa, Nigeria, Egypt,

From 2010 – 2017, 44 women led nations. From 2018 – 2023 the number exploded to more than 50.

44 Women

Women Prime Ministers and Presidents are now common-place in Europe and Asia.

30 Women

The 1990s saw an explosion of women leaders from all walks of life.

35 Women

Women have led nations on every continent.

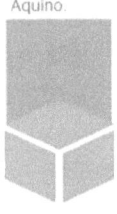

9 Women

4 Asian, 2 European, 2 S. American and 1 from Africa take the helm

9 Women

In an age of legendary women like Thatcher, and Aquino.

1970s **1980s** **1990s** **2000s** **2010s**

CHAPTER 7. WOMEN LEADERS OF EUROPE

41

URSULA GERTRUD VON DER LEYEN
European Union President 2019 – present.

Ursula was born into a German family involved in Saxony and German leadership in politics. After a two track education she returned to politics and served in a variety of local, state and national positions. Considered one of the logical choices to follow Chancellor Angela Merkel because of her portfolio as Defense Minister of Germany from 2013 – 2019. She presided over a period of rebuilding outdated military equipment and the upheaval from the Russian invasion of Ukraine and the refuges crisis from the middle east. An extra focus was placed on German military readiness to respond to the Russian threat and emerging terrorist threats. While she was the

---

[41] Wikipedia Commons.

primary advocate for modernizing the German arsenal, she was also blamed for the lack of readiness.[42]

When the election to replace Merkel occurred she did not offer herself as a candidate. At the super-nation level, the European Union's executive branch elections were a mess and finally were resolved by a series of negotiated compromises and candidates which led to her surprise nomination for European Union President, which she narrowly won.

During her terms she focused on gender equality within the E.U, the threat of climate change and the two major emergencies that affected the continent, the Covid virus and the second Russian invasion of Ukraine. In both cases she formulated a robust, active and well financed response to the threat to help defeat the virus and help the Ukrainians defend their homeland from the Russian Dictator Putin. She continues to serve in this capacity with distinction to this day.

---

[42] https://www.britannica.com/biography/Ursula-von-der-Leyen

ROBERTA METSOLA
President of the European Parliament 2022 – present.

A lawyer from the island nation of Malta, Roberta and her husband were the first European couple to run for the European Parliament from different countries, and lose. Thgough devasted, they both ran again, making an agreement that if one won their election, the other would stay at home and take care of their young child. Roberta won her election in 2013 and her husband, Ukko, kept his word and retired from politics. After representing Malta in the European Parliament for several terms. She served on a civil liberties committee and in that capacity worked and wrote extensively on how the EU should overcome homophobia and how it should properly and

---

43 Wikipedia Commons.

humanely handle the refugee crisis. As a result, she was elected to the Vice-President of the European Parliament in 2020, and when the President became ill, she was chosen to succeed him as President of the EU Parliament in 2022, the youngest person ever elected to the position. In that capacity she has worked against corruption. She is also known for her anti-abortion stance, though she respects the laws of the EU protecting the legal right to it, personally does not agree with the practice.

VJOSA OSMANI
President of Kosovo 2021 – present.

As a teenager during the Kosovo War, a Serbian soldier had forced the barrel of an AK 47 into her mouth as he threatened to kill her when they invaded her home. She studied Law in the US at the University of Pittsburgh. In 2009 she served as Chief of Staff and Legal Counsel to the then President of Kosovo. Then she was elected to the Assembly in her own right for three terms. She represented the President at the Constitutional Convention to write the Kosovo Constitution and represented Kosovo in the International Court of Justice in defense of Kosovo's legal standing as an independent nation. She holds strong opinions on who her party LDK should form coalitions with, she clashed with leadership and was removed from the leadership and resigned the party in 2019. Ironically, by

---

[44] Wikimedia Commons.

2020, she was appointed acting President due to a scandal and resignation. She formed her own political party Guxo and ran against corruption winning a landslide to become President in her own right. The LDK party she left faired poorly. As President she looks to reconcile with Serbia while expecting that Serbia will at some point apologize for starting the war and genocide in kosovo.[45]

[45] https://en.wikipedia.org/wiki/Vjosa_Osmani

KAJA KALLAS
Prime Minister of Estonia 2021 – present.

The daughter of a former Estonian Prime Minister, Siim Kallas, and her great grandfather was one of the Founding Fathers who helped Estonia gain its independence in 1918. Her mother's family was deported to Siberia during the Soviet rule of Estonia. She studied

---

46 Wikimedia Commons.

business and law and it was only natural that she gravitated to politics, being elected first to the Estonian Parliament from 2011 – 2014 and then to the European Union Parliament from 2014 – 2018. She focused on the technology sector and protecting businesses and consumers. Considered a powerhouse throughout Europe on tech issues, she rose to lead the Reform Party from 2017 to 2020, when she was elevated to the Prime Minister's office, the first woman in Estonia's history, after a scandal had sidelined her predecessor. [47]

The energy crisis and the Russian invasion of Ukraine have dominated her term. At first she tried to let the free market correct the high oil and gas prices which proved to be unpopular. However, her firm stance against Putin's Russian invasion of Ukraine saw her regain her popularity. She made immediately available materials to aid the Ukrininans in their fight against the aggression, she also lobbied to admit Ukraine to the European Union, a bold and courageous position. In her second term, she continued her strong support of Ukraine and passed legislation legalizing same sex marriage and adoption. She was widely discussed as a possible next NATO Secretary General. In 2023 a scandal broke regarding stock her husband owned of a company that was still doing business in trade-embargoed Russia. The apparent conflict of interest tarnished her reputation but did not lead her to resign. [48]

---

[47] By U.S. Department of State from United States - Secretary Blinken Meets With Estonian Prime Minister Kallas, Public Domain, https://commons.wikimedia.org/w/index.php?curid=115971163
[48] https://en.wikipedia.org/wiki/Kaja_Kallas

SANNA MARIN
Prime Minister Finland 2019 – 2023.

Elected Prime Minister of Finland at the young age of 34, she was confronted with the Covid crisis and Russian invasion of neighboring Ukraine almost immediately. She boldly closed Finland's borders and schools which led to the quick containment of the disease and

---

49 Wikimedia Commons.

allowed Finland to recover quicker than elsewhere. Finland shares an 800 mile long border with Russia and for 70 years had been neutral, but upon the Putin invasion of Ukraine, Marin immediately filed for NATO membership seeing the danger that happened to Ukraine could easily be in store for Finland. Her efficient and courageous handling of both Covid and the Russian threat are hallmarks of her administration.

When a video leaked of her dancing and having fun with her friends in private, conservatives in Finland were harsh in their criticism. But Marin, who manages her own Instagram account, defended herself and struck a chord with many people.

"I am a human. During these dark times, I too need some joy, light and fun." She was seen by most as a normal person dancing and having fun. Thousands of people flooded the internet with videos of themselves dancing in support of her.

Born into a family with two moms, she feels strongly that leaders of countries should be just normal people. She claims her never aspired to the Prime Minister position, but that as she rose to Deputy Prime Minister, when he had to resign she asked herself: 'If someone else can do it, why not me.' Why not indeed. She narrowly lost re-election due to an anti-immigration backlash which made the conservative parties the more popular choice.[50]

---

[50] https://www.cbsnews.com/news/sanna-marin-finland-60-minutes-2023-02-19/

METTE FREDERIKSEN
Prime Minister of Denmark 2019 – present.

Mette began her political career at the young age of 15, at 24 she was elected to Parliament and became her party's spokesperson.During Helle Thorning-Schmidt's term as the first female Prime Minister for Denmark, Mette served as Cabinet Secretary for Employment, the later Secretary for Justice. After that term was over she served as

---

[51] Wikipedia.

Leader of the opposition party until the Social Democrats won again in 2019 and she became Prime Minister.[52]

As Prime Minister she has thrown the full weight of her support behind Ukraine after the Russian invasion. She has pushed for the normally non-military minded Denmark to set aside 2% of its spending to increase its military capability, in case NATO has to engage with Russia. Her strong stance also made her a potential candidate to head NATO.[53]

---

[52] https://www.councilwomenworldleaders.org/mette-frederiksen.html
[53] https://www.reuters.com/world/denmarks-tough-lady-play-new-nato-chief-ahead-white-house-visit-2023-06-02/

MAGDALENA ANDERSSON
President of Sweden 2021 – 2022.

A champion swimmer in her youth, Andersson received a PhD in Economics and became an advisor to the Swedish President in 1996. She rose to Director of Planning, to Finance Minister during the 2000s. From 2009 – 2012 she served as the Director of the Swedish Tax Agency and again Minister of Finance from 2014 – 2021 for yet another Swedish President. She was known for her bluntness and no-nonsense approach and ran a strong economy with low inflation and low unemployment.

---

[54] Facebook, Magdalena Andersson Profile.

She had a remarkable beginning to her term as Prime Minister resigning 7 hours after her term begun out of principle because the Parliament had voted down her budget. She returned a few days later to preside over a budget that passed. Her priorities for the first years in office were a commitment to reversing the privitization of schools, a commitment to be a model nation for climate control policies and to end the practice of segregating immigrants from the general Swedish population, a practice begun under Covid restrictions.[55]

---

[55] https://www.britannica.com/biography/Magdalena-Andersson

INGRIDA SIMONYTE
Prime Minister of Lithuania 2020 -present.

Simonyte was an economist who worked for 20 years in finance to lead the Finance Minister in 2009. After a brief stint in private banking she was elected to Parliament in 2018. After one term, she ran for Prime Minister and polled second, however her party joined a coalition which constituted a majority and, as a result, she was asked to serve as Prime Minister. Her term was typified by a swift and effectie response to Covid, and to several successful strategic works projects including investments in education, tech sectors, streamlining government efficiency and stabilizing the energy grid specifically because of the Russian war in Ukraine.[57]

---

[56] Wikimedia Commons.
[57] https://en.wikipedia.org/wiki/Ingrida_%C5%A0imonyt%C4%97

58

QUEEN ELIZABETH II
Reign 1952 -2022.

No discussion of 20th – 21st Century Women Leaders of Nations would be complete without including the important role of Queen Elizabeth II's 70 year rule. In the initial installments of this publication the storied Queen was not included because it featured

---

58 Wikimedia.

only women Presidents and Prime Ministers. This publication includes select women leaders at the U.N, the E.U and other leaders of peoples, like the Ambassador for the 35 million worldwide refugees and others. As the number of women Presidents and Prime Ministers exploded between the second edition and this third edition from 108 in total to more than 150 in just five years, it made impractical covering the biography of every single temporary, accidental, transitional, elevated and appointed and sometimes ceremonial women leaders. So, many women leaders who have served in a tempory capacity were not included. The smallest of nations leaders were set aside in favor of more impactful and influential women leaders.

Queen Elizabeth II's rule defines much of the world's story in the 20th Century. When she took the throne, the 27 year old royal ruled over 700 million people, nearly one-third of the world's population. The sun truly never set on the British Empire at that moment in time. Yet slowly as the majority of those nations began to yearn for more autonomy, freedom and independence, she managed to slowly extricate the massive empire from these fledgling states yearning to be free. Often with a minimum of bloodshed, she tacitly gave her blessings to many of the new nations and actively tried to offer a second type of new independence, the commonwealth. By allowing nations their independence but keeping them bound to Great Britain through the Commonwealth of States she bound their economies to her ever shrinking empire. I have often wondered whether a man, a King, in such a predicament would not have made the mistake of trying to hang on to each colony through brute force. The Queen, though never to be confused with a warm mothering type, acted like a mother would with her children growing up and leaving, she reluctantly let them go, bade them well but kept the ties that bound them in tact, cleverly, with many of them through the British Commonwealth. Like having her children live close by or work for the family company.

ANGELA MERKEL

1st Woman Elected Chancellor of Germany
2005 – 2021.[ccii]

"Let us answer the terrorists by living our values with courage."[cciii]

Angela Merkel grew up in a theological household in the Communist dictatorship of East Germany during the Cold War. She studied

Quantum Chemistry in College. When the Berlin wall came down, she was, for a time, a spokesperson for the first and only democratically-elected government of East Germany (also led by a woman – Sabine Bergmann-Pohl). [cciv]

In 1990, Merkel was elected to the Bundestag, the national Parliament. She was appointed Minister for Women and Youth in the early 1990s and a few years later, Minister for the Environment. She was considered a gangly and awkward politician at first but her straightforward approach quickly garnered her respect. When her party was out of power, she rose quickly to become its leader in 2000. The confusing 2005 election result helped lead to a compromise government that brought Merkel to power as Chancellor in a coalition. [ccv]

In 2013, she won re-election with another coalition government. The characteristics of her terms in office and her highest achievements were:

> She helped manage the 2007-2008 economic crisis for Germany and for the entire E.U.
> Introduced Germany's first minimum wage.
> Approved the phase out of Germany's fleet of aging nuclear power plants.
> Approved maternity and paternity pay. [ccvi]
> She led the Greek bail outs of 2010, 2012, and 2015 keeping the economic cohesion of the E.U. [ccvii]

- She played a pivotal role in the Lisbon Treaty, a crucial environmental treaty.
- She served as President of the European Council, one of the E. U's executive branches comprised of the Presidents and Prime Ministers of every E.U nation.
- 2015 Time 'Person of the Year' and 2016 Forbes 'Most Powerful Woman in the World' for her tenth time! [ccviii]

DALIA GRYBAUSKAITE

1st Woman Elected President of Lithuania
2009 – Present.

"The problem is that Putin's Russia today is ready and willing to go to war. Europe and the West are not ready and willing to go to war. Afterwards, we will be surprised that new territories are taken, that new countries are partitioned." [ccix ccx]

---

[59] Wikimedia Commons.

"I am to a staggering degree straight to the point and direct."[ccxi]

Dalia Grybauskaite played basketball and worked her way through College as a factory worker in St. Petersburg. After graduation, she was a secretary and a High School teacher. She joined the Soviet Communist Party during the 1980s and was a member of the Lithuanian Communist Party until 1990. [ccxii] From 2004 – 2009, she was Vice-Minister of Foreign Affairs and Minister of Finance and served as European Commissioner for Financial Programming and the Budget. [ccxiii] She received 69% of the Presidential vote in 2009 and 58% of the vote in 2014. She advocated successfully for boycotting the Russian Sochi Olympics in protest of recent Russian aggression and its poor human rights record. She is one of the few Eastern European voices that have strongly criticized Putin and Russia's invasion of the Ukraine and has called Russia a "terrorist state," warning that Russian aggression "could spread throughout Europe." [ccxiv]

On Russia, Grybauskaite is firm:

"We are so busy trying not to offend Putin, who is today sending his troops to kill and occupy Ukrainian territory. Why are we not sensitive about what Ukrainians are feeling?"[ccxv]

ERNA SOLBERG
Prime Minister of Norway
2013 – 2021.

Diagnosed with dyslexia at 16, Solberg overcame learning difficulties to be elected to the Student Union of Norway. In 1979, she was elected as a Deputy Member of the Bergen City Council and to the Storting in 1989, the Norwegian Parliament. [ccxvi] In 2001, she became the Minister for Local Government and Regional Development. Her tough stance on immigration asylum seekers earned her the nickname, 'Iron Erna.' She later reversed this position. As Prime Minister, recently, she has been in the news for playing *Pokemon Go* during a session of Parliament. [ccxvii] Solberg has been skewered in the press and online for the 'Pokemon Go Incident' but has taken it with humor.

---

[60] Photo Source: Wikiwand

NICOLA STURGEON
1st Female First (Prime) Minister – Scotland
(not independent), 2014 – 2023.

"When somebody is diagnosed with a terrible illness, my instinct is to view them as a human being, not consider what country they came from."

A lawyer and lifelong politician, Sturgeon assumed the leadership of Scotland after PM Salmond stepped down following the Brexit vote. She has indicated that Scotland would consider removing itself from Great Britain if Britain does, in fact, exit the EU because of the potential negative economic consequences Brexit it would have on Scotland.

---

[61] Photo Credit: Wikimedia Commons.

62

BEATO SZYDLO
Prime Minister of Poland
2015 – 2017.

Born to a coal mining family, Beata Szydlo became a Mayor at the early age of 35. She joined the Law and Justice Party, where she rose to become a deputy leader. [ccxviii] In September 2005, she was elected to Parliament and was appointed vice-chairman of the Law and Justice party in 2010. Four years later, she became the Treasurer of the Law and Justice party. [ccxix] After her management of President Duda's campaign, she was named as a candidate for the office of Prime Minister. In 2015, she was invited the President of Poland to form a government.[ccxx] Her administration's goals are to reduce the retirement age and raise the minimum wage throughout Poland.

---

[62] Wikimedia Creative Commons.

KOLINDA GRABAR-KITAROVIC
First Woman Elected President of Croatia
2015 – Present.

"Sometimes I had to work harder than men and I have been subject to misogyny. But my battle is one for equality, not just for women. I am not a feminist...I just want equal opportunities for everyone." [ccxxi] [ccxxii]

Kolinda Grabar-Kitarović was elected the first female President of Croatia in 2015 and was also the youngest Croatian President ever elected.

She began her career as an advisor to the International Cooperation Department of the Ministry of Science and Technology. From 1995 – 1997, she directed the North American division of the Croatian Foreign Ministry. She was first elected to the Croatian Parliament in 2003 and became the Minister of Foreign Affairs. In 2008, she was appointed to the high-profile position of Croatian Ambassador to the

---

[63] Wikimedia Commons.

U.S. and also served as Assistant Secretary General for Public Diplomacy at NATO. [ccxxiii]

With a new administration, she served as Croatia's Minister of European Integration which oversaw crucial NATO and E.U integration. When she won election to the Presidency in 2015, she became only the second woman in history to defeat an incumbent President and the first conservative to be elected in Croatia in fifteen years.

64

Her administration is currently occupied with the Syrian refugee crisis. Though most refugees pass through Croatia to other destinations, tens of thousands have remained in her nation creating a crisis confronting her Presidency.

---

[64] Wikimedia Commons.

THERESA MAY
Prime Minister of Great Britain
2016 – 2019.

After the Brexit vote ended the career of Prime Minister Cameron, Theresa May was elected head of the Conservative Party and was elevated as the second female Prime Minister of Great Britain.

---

[65] Wikimedia Commons.

As a child, she enjoyed pantomime and worked in a bakery. She also wanted to be the first British woman to be Prime Minister and in College was reportedly irritated when Margaret Thatcher beat her to it. At Oxford University, she was introduced to her future husband by future Pakistani Prime Minister Benazir Bhutto, who was also a student there. After graduation, she went to work at the Bank of England and became the Director of the European Affairs Department at the bank.

She is known for her serious, no-nonsense demeanor. Labor MP Yvette Cooper, described her: "I respect her style - it is steady and serious. She is authoritative in parliament - superficial attacks on her bounce off." [ccxxiv]

May has confirmed her commitment to removing Britain from the E.U because of the Brexit vote. "Brexit means Brexit," there will be no second referendum on the issue. [ccxxv] May called for snap elections to strengthen her hand in Parliament in mid-2017. This backfired as she lost her ruling majority, in part due to a spate of terrorist attacks. But she was able to barely sustain her government. It is rumored that her new weaker position may lead to the end of her term as Prime Minister.

In recent interviews, May has showed a bit of her personal life, disclosing she has Type 1 diabetes, indicating she would choose a lifetime subscription to Vogue as the luxury item she would take to a deserted island. She also collects cookbooks and is a fan of ABBA and Mozart.

KERSTI KALJULAID

1st Woman Elected President of Estonia
2016 – Present.

An excerpt of Kersti Kaljulaid's powerful inauguration speech October 10th, 2016, on the 25th Anniversary of Estonia's Independence.

"Today's children only know about the occupation as part of the memories of their grandparents. They are the grandchildren of a free Estonia. Today I think about these children – and of their grandchildren. But indeed, how small is the number of these children. Babies sleep in cots in fewer than fifteen thousand Estonian homes. Approximately one hundred thousand preschool children are there to sneak into their parents' beds in the morning. All over the world there are hundreds of millions of such children.

Self-confidence is a pre-requisite and important foundation for development and success. Those small children I think about today, as I stand here – they are self-confident. They have immense faith in us, but they also have the same immense faith in themselves.

A president of a democratic country cannot single-handedly create a fair, caring environment that supports self-confidence. A president can only articulate and see that important issues for our children and grandchildren – and their children – will always be on the agenda. The president is responsible for the Estonia of our children and grandchildren. An Estonia of self-confident, well-educated and healthy people. It is the job of the president to remember that an ethical state must offer opportunities to the strong and support to the weak. But this is the task for us, the people here, in this hall, today. The self-confidence and courage to act in the interests of our children and grandchildren. Their education. Their health, and the health and well-being of our parents. The care that we exhibit in looking after our parents today will show our children how they should take care of us once they are grown up. The time will continue to pass and indeed the future will inevitably come, even if we don't think about it every day. However, the rightful, bold decisions we take today will help ensure that the hope in the eyes of those looking at us from their cradles will be fulfilled. To present and future generations, as is stated in the constitution.

Let us cherish Estonia!" [ccxxvi]

Kaljulaid is a former genetic biologist, investment banker and sales manager. From 1999 to 2002, she worked as the economic advisor of

Estonian Prime Minister Mart Laar, then went on to direct an Estonian power plant from 2002 to 2004, the first woman to do so in Estonia.[ccxxvii] When Estonia joined the European Union in 2004, she was appointed the country's representative at the European Court of Auditors. [ccxxviii] Since 2011, Kaljulaid has been the chairperson of the board of the University of Tartu.

After a deadlocked Presidential election in 2016, Kaljulaid was brought in as a compromise candidate. Her non-aligned status, and her tech and security minded platform won the field. [ccxxix] She is known for her liberal views on LGBT rights, and her commitment to cyber-security.

The youthful and stylistic Kaljulaid is already a grandmother.

ATIFETE JAHJAGA
1st Woman President of Kosovo
2011 – 2016.

"Women are ... agents of peace, of conflict resolution, of state-building, and their direct involvement ensures a safer and a more just world for everyone. It is imperative and smart to include talented women in the equation to find solutions to our common challenges."

Jahjaga began her career as a policewoman when Kosovo established its first police force in 2000. She served as Deputy Director of the Police of Kosovo, as Major General, a position she was appointed to in February of 2009. [ccxxx]

She became one of the youngest head of state in the world when she took office in 2011 at age 36. As President, she built international relationships, raised the profile of Kosovo, fought for women's empowerment, and advocated for Kosovo's admission into the European Union. As President, she successfully advocated for reparations for the 20,000 rape victims from the Kosovo War. [ccxxxi]

68

A quote on **living through the Kosovo and Bosnian Wars."** *It was a horrible situation, (my generation) was not allowed to live our own life. We were not allowed to live like our peers from that time in the region or in Europe. We were simply not allowed to dream big because we didn't know what was going to happen tomorrow."*

---

[68] Wikimedia Commons

LAIMDOTA STRAUJUMA
Latvian Prime Minister 2014 – 2016.

"We have three priorities, a competitive Europe, a digital Europe and an engaged Europe."

Strajuma is an economist who served in a variety of posts in the Ministry of Agriculture until she was elevated to Agriculture Minister in 2011. [ccxxxii] In 2014, she was elected Prime Minister after her party's coalition won a majority. Her candidacy was supported by several parties in a grand coalition. [ccxxxiii] It was a difficult time for Latvia and the ruling coalition. The troubles included: the Russian invasion of Ukraine, the Syrian refugee crisis, a 2% NATO fund allocation and the rescue of the national economy. The coalition collapsed after two years. [ccxxxiv]

---

[69] Creative Commons.

HELLE THORNING-SCHMIDT
1st Female Prime Minister of Denmark, 2011 – 2015.

"Peace and solidarity in Europe is not a law of nature. It requires caring, effort and perseverance."

Thorning-Schmidt's rise to Denmark's leadership began in the mid-1990s when she represented the Social Democrats in the European Parliament (the Parliament within the E.U). She worked with trade unions in Denmark until her election to the Danish Parliament in 1999. [ccxxxv] She quickly rose to the leadership of her party and because her party was the largest of the left of center opposition parties, she was largely considered to be the head of the opposition. [ccxxxvi] In

---

[70] Wikipedia Commons. Both images.

2011, the center-left parties became a majority in Parliament and so Thorning-Schmidt was asked to form a government.

"I just thought it was a bit fun. Maybe it also shows that when we meet heads of state and government, we too are just people who have fun."

In her term as the first female Prime Minister of Denmark, she famously posed for a 'selfie' with U.S President Obama and British Prime Minister Cameron during the funeral ceremonies for Nelson Mandela. After her coalition's defeat in 2015, she resigned as Prime Minister and retired from politics. [ccxxxvii] After leaving politics, she continued working in the field of human rights and humanitarian aid. Thorning-Schmidt is the current Director of Save the Children.

Characteristics of her two terms as Prime Minister are:

➢ Relaxing immigration restrictions.
➢ Lowered taxes for the top income brackets.
➢ Completed the Danish part in the NATO bombing of Libya.
➢ Sold the Danish national energy stake to Goldman Sachs. [ccxxxviii]

JOHANNA SIGURDARDOTTIR
World's 1st Openly GLBT Prime Minister
1st Female Prime Minister of Iceland 2009 – 2013.

"The Nordic countries are leading the way on women's equality, recognizing women as equal citizens rather than commodities for sale."

Sigurdardóttir was a flight attendant and airline union organizer before diving into the world of politics. She was elected to the

Althingi, the Icelandic Parliament, from 1978 until 2009, when she was elected the first female Prime Minister of Iceland.

Sigurdardóttir as a stewardess and with her partner. Photo credits: myholyoak and aaniran.bogspot.co

She held Ministerial positions in different Cabinets and was the longest-serving member of the Althingi. She had the credibility to be appointed Interim Prime Minister during the financial crisis of 2008 that bankrupted Iceland and forced the resignation of Prime Minister Geir Haarde. [ccxl]

She is the first openly LGBT leader in the world to head a national government and the first female Prime Minister of Iceland. She advanced LGBT rights, human rights and social justice during her term. She and her partner are both divorced mothers and wed each other in 2002 immediately after the Icelandic passage of the marriage equality law. [ccxli]

TARJA HALONEN
1st Woman President of Finland
2000 – 2012.

"(We) can only thrive when women of learning, in common with their male counterparts, are guaranteed the opportunity to use their creativity to the full." cxlii

After studying Art History in College, and then law, Halonen began her career as a union lawyer in 1970. In 1974 the Finnish Prime Minister appointed her as his Parliamentary Secretary. Her elected

---

71 Wikimedia Commons.

career began as a local City Council member for twenty years in Helsinki, the Finnish Capital. She was simultaneously elected to and served in the Finnish Parliament in 1979. In the late 1980s she was appointed Minister of Social Affairs and in the early 1990s she served as Minister of Justice. [ccxliii]

Halonen had a longstanding reputation within her party of being very hard working and she was an easy choice for her party and voters when the President from her party retired. In 2000 she won the run-off and dominated the election becoming Finland's first female President. Re-elected in 2006 she served her term through 2012. Halonen is known for her commitment to human rights and gay rights. [ccxliv]

She is credited with being a strong proponent the E.U, human rights and protection of people marginalized by globalization.

IVETA RADICOVA
1st Woman Prime Minister of Slovakia
2010 – 2012.

"In some countries, we have the right to vote for less than 100 years, so the entry of women into political leadership has caused a tsunami."

Iveta Radicova graduated from Oxford University and was married to the late Slovakian comedian Stano Radic. She jumped into politics as the spokesperson for the political party 'Public against Violence' in the early 1990s. [ccxlvi] She briefly served as the Minister of Labor in the mid-2000s and was elected to Parliament in 2006. Due to her party's

(SDKU-DS) weak election showing, it became the opposition and she was elected to her party's leadership.[ccxlvii]

In 2009, Radicova was picked as her party's nominee for President; she also garnered the endorsement of two smaller parties. This gave her a surprisingly strong showing in the first round of voting with 38%. She qualified for the runoff and narrowly lost the general election with 44.5%. [ccxlviii]

She stepped down from all political office after the defeat and some minor Parliamentary rule controversy. [ccxlix] But her party was not finished with her. The SDKU-DS voted her in as its leader during the Parliamentary elections in 2010. Their platform revolved around fiscal responsibility, and while they lost the Parliamentary elections, the party that won, SMER, was unable to cobble together a ruling coalition. As head of the largest opposition party, Radicova was asked to put together a government.[ccl] During her term, she negotiated the EU stabilization bailout plan for Slovakia. The small nation's financial contribution to it was staggering and unpopular. However, it provided much needed aid and helped place Slovakia's economy on firmer footing. Unfortunately, as a result, Radicova's popularity plummeted and her government was voted out. She declined to stand for office again. [ccli]

MARY McALEESE
President of Ireland
1997 – 2011.

"It is absolutely no coincidence that peace and reconciliation that eluded us for hundreds of years, has at last come to pass in an Ireland where the talents of women are now flooding every aspect of life as never before."[xlii]

---

[72] Wikimedia Creative Commons.

In 1994, she became the first Pro-Chancellor of Queen's University. She was one of five female candidates for President in 1997. She won and was the first person elected President of Ireland from North Ireland. The characteristics of her terms in office were a commitment to repairing divisions within Ireland, improving the system of justice and better social inclusion. [ccliii] After her terms in office, she remained popular in Ireland, despite the small controversies of her terms. [ccliv]
[cclv]

YULIA TYMOSHENKO

1st Woman Prime Minister of Ukraine
Co-Leader of The Orange Revolution
2005, 2007 – 2010.

"My goal in politics has been, and will be, the goal of giving Ukraine a chance to finally secure firm footing in the world as a competitive, independent and real European state."

In a newly independent Ukraine, Tymoshenko was the Director of the United Energy Systems of Ukraine and served as the Energy Minister from 1999 - 2001. In 2004, in a pivotal election about the fundamental direction of Ukraine, the Yanukovych-pro-Russian side attempted to steal the election and Tymoshenko emerged as a powerful voice against voter fraud. This triggered the 'Orange Revolution.' She would spellbind huge crowds and helped overturn the results ensuring the election of Victor Yushchenko the pro-Western candidate. [cclvi]

In 2005, she was appointed Prime Minister to President Yushchenko, but they soon clashed. Her government was quickly dismissed by Yushchenko. However she was re-elected Prime Minister in 2007 by a bare majority of lawmakers. Relations between the two remained very rocky and he attempted to dismiss her new government several times but never had enough votes. Tymoshenko was known for calling for Ukraine to join NATO and for opposing Russian aggression in Georgia. In face to face meetings though, Putin claimed to respect her. Ironically, Tymoshenko ran against pro-Russian Yanukovych for the Presidency in 2010, and narrowly lost. Criminal charges were immediately brought against her and she was found guilty and jailed for a gas deal with Russia. The case was politically motivated. Her health began to fail and in 2014 and she was released by Parliament after a revolution swept Yanukovych from power. All charges against her were retroactively removed. She remains a power in Ukraine.

JADRANKA KOSOR

Prime Minister of Croatia
2009 – 2011.

Jadranka Kosor began her career as a journalist and hosted a radio show about the human side of the Bosnian War. At the end of the war, she was elevated to Vice-President of Croatian Democratic Union Political Party. Her party enjoyed a string of election victories in the early 2000s and she served as Minister of Family and Veteran's Affairs and Deputy Prime Minister. [cclvii]

She was her party's standard bearer in 2005 but lost in the general election for President. In 2009 after the resignation of the incumbent Prime Minister, Kosor was able to build a majority coalition and became Prime Minister, only to be swept out of power less than two years later in 2011. [cclviii] [cclix] Her term was known for her country's crackdown on political and business corruption which, ironically, led to the arrest of prominent members of her own party.

She is credited with Croatia's crucial admission to the E.U and resolving a border dispute peacefully with Slovenia. [cclx] After her election loss, she also lost control of the leadership of her party.

cclxi ZINAIDA GRECEANII

Prime Minister of Moldova 2008 – 2009.

Zinaida Greceanii was born in Siberia, Russia, to parents who had been exiled from Moldova for their religion during one of the Soviet purges. Shortly after she was born, they returned to Moldova. When Greceanii became involved in politics, she migrated from the Communist Party to the Socialist Party of Moldova. [cclxii] In 2000 she was elevated to Deputy Minister of Finance, and Minister of Finance in 2002. [cclxiii] She held this high-profile position until she was elected Prime Minister in 2005. The election results were deemed invalid because of low voter turnout. But in 2008, the sitting Prime Minister resigned and she was appointed. [cclxiv]

Her government focused on freedom of the media and the independence of the Judiciary. She increasing the number of women Ministers from two to five. [cclxv] In the 2009 election, she came excruciatingly close to becoming President, falling one vote short of the 61 necessary. In a 2nd round of voting she had 48% of the vote and the opposition was asked to form a coalition government. [cclxvi]

cclxvii

VAIRA VIKE-FREIBERGA

1st Woman President of Latvia 1997 – 2007.

"It's easier to tolerate a dictator when he is dictating someone else's life."

Vike-Freiberga's family fled Latvia during the World War Two and she was raised in refugee camps in Germany and Morocco. When she immigrated to Canada, she worked as a bank teller and attended the University of Toronto and McGill. As a Psychologist, she wrote numerous books and taught at the University of Montreal. When she returned to independent Latvia, she was appointed Director of the Latvian Institute. After a deadlocked election, she was elected President of Latvia because of her neutrality. She:

- ➢ Supervised Latvia's ascension to NATO.
- ➢ Oversaw Latvia's Membership to the European Union.

177

cclxviii **NINO BURJANADZE**

1st Woman Prime Minister of Georgia 2004, 2007.
Leader of the Rose Revolution

After the collapse of the Soviet Union, the Republic of Georgia elected former Soviet Foreign Minister Shevardnadze as its President for ten years until the 2003 election. In 2003, the President's party committed election fraud which triggered the 'Rose Revolution.' The opposition stormed the government buildings armed with nothing more than roses. Burjanadze was part of the troika of leadership who led the Rose Revolution. She stood in front of tens of thousands of people, during the protests and helped roll back the anarchy that engulfed her nation. As a result, the 38-year-old Burjanadze was chosen to lead a transitional government to bring about a free and fair election. As promised, she stepped down after the elections. She was called on once again in 2007 to perform the same task. Her selfless action helped stabilize Georgia during a time of great upheaval and uncertainty. cclxix

cclxx

RADMILLA SEKERINSKA

Youngest Woman Prime Minister in the Modern Age
1st Woman Prime Minister of Macedon, 2004

"Macedonian citizens have long waited for an end to the crisis and have long known that the first step to ending it is fair and democratic elections, nothing more, nothing less."cclxxi

Radmila Sekerinska entered politics by winning a seat on the Skopje City Council (the Capital of Macedonia) at the very young age of 24. She worked at the Faculty of Electric Engineering while starting her

179

political career. She was elected to Parliament in 1998 at 26 years old, where her rise was meteoric.

She quickly rose to the Deputy Chair to the SDSM, the largest political party at the time. [cclxxii] After serving on several Parliamentary Committees, she was appointed VP of Macedonian integration into the E.U, a very important and high profile post. [cclxxiii]

When the sitting Prime Minister won the presidential election, she was asked to fill in as Prime Minister as he prepared his Cabinet. She did so, briefly, twice in 2004 at the very young age of 32, the youngest female Prime Minister in modern history. When she stepped down, she became the Deputy Prime Minister. [cclxxiv]

In April of 2017, Sekerinska was assaulted on the floor of the Parliament when nationalist thug stormed the floor. Other politicians were also assaulted. She escaped serious injury. Her name and accomplishments were rarely mentioned in press reports of the incident, instead, much of the media referred to her assault as 'a woman was pulled to the floor by her hair.'

NATASA MICIC

1st Woman President of Serbia
2002 – 2004.

"Maybe they thought I wouldn't be strong enough to stand up to them because I am a woman. They were wrong. We need more women in politics, most importantly in elected positions. It's time for women to get involved to protect their interests."

In 2002, Natasa Micic was constitutionally elevated to the Office of the Presidency from the position of President of the National Assembly after two rounds of Presidential elections failed to receive the required minimum number of votes. Her role as Speaker of the

181

Parliament was designated to fill a vacancy in the Presidential Office, so she was elevated to the Presidency during the impasse. At the time, Serbia was still the primary state in the fragmenting Yugoslavian Federation. At the young age of 37 she became President and presided over a period when the new Serbian Constitution was written and the new Serbian state was being created. [cclxxvii] During her term, she prolonged the re-election and declared a temporary state of emergency. [cclxxviii] Serbia became a single, independent state in 2006.

Only two years before becoming President of Serbia, she and a friend were leading anti-Milosevic protests in a car labeled 'Thelma and Louise!' Her youthful demeanor and straightforward honesty redefined what it was to be a modern President.

An Excerpt from a 2002 interview by Dejan Anastasijevic for Time Europe Magazine.

"Do you feel like an accidental President?"
"I do. This is a job for an elected official, and I was not elected. I see this as a temporary solution – just until new elections."

Does the speed of your progress make you nervous?
"Of course, it does. A new job is always a stressful thing, and this is the top job. However, I am certain I'm up to it."

MARY ROBINSON
1st Woman President of Ireland
1990 – 1997.

"Human rights are inscribed in the hearts of people; they were there long before lawmakers drafted their first proclamation."
cclxxix

Mary Robinson was a Law Professor for 22 years at her Alma Mater Trinity College Law and became the Chancellor of the School. She also served as a Senator for 20 years until 1989. As a lawyer, she argued important human rights cases in front of the European Court of Human Rights. cclxxx

She was elected President of Ireland and served two terms from 1990 – 1997. She raised the profile of the Presidency and bravely visited Somalia and Rwanda in the immediate aftermath of violence and genocide there. Her term and her career has been dedicated to human rights.

After her term, she continued working for worldwide human rights as the UN High Commissioner for Human Rights from 1997 – 2002. Her groundbreaking visits included the first UNHCHR visit to China.[cclxxxi] She has served on many UN panels and missions and received many top honors from around the world for her work in human rights.

---

[74] Photo Source: Health and Human Resources Journal

HANNA SUCHOCKA
1st Woman Polish Prime Minister
1992 – 1993.

"I am not linked with any feminist movement. But there exists some kind of women's solidarity." [cclxxxii]

After law school, Hanna Suchocka worked as a researcher at a local University but she was fired when she refused to join the Communist

Party and instead joined the Democratic Party. She continued her studies in West Germany during the 1970s and was elected to the Polish Parliament, the Sejm, in 1980.[cclxxxiii] During her terms in Parliament she became a legal advisor to Solidarity, the powerful pro-union, pro-independence Polish workers' movement. [cclxxxiv] In 1981, she stood up to the regime by voting against the imposition of Martial Law, in the crackdown against Solidarity. She was forced to resign from Parliament by the regime. She was re-elected to Parliament with the support of Solidarity. [cclxxxv]

Her understated nature made her an unlikely candidate for Prime Minister in 1992, so she surprised many observers when she beat out an entirely male field of contenders. She was known for keeping a low profile. [cclxxxvi] She created a stir by firing her Minister of Finance for being habitually late to meetings.[cclxxxvii] Her term was brief, though longer than the ones that proceeded her. She led her country in its first steps toward a free market and attempted to create a national dialogue of reconciliation between vastly different views. When talks broke down with strikers, Poland was paralyzed. [cclxxxviii] Her leadership did not survive a vote of no confidence.

She later founded a new political party which quickly became one of the top powers in the country. She also served as Minister of Justice in a coalition government in the late 1990s, and Ambassador. [cclxxxix]

Her time as Prime Minister was pivotal to Poland's relatively peaceful transition from a military, Soviet-aligned dictatorship to a free, liberal democracy. Fun fact: Suchocka's grandmother was a member of the first Polish Parliament of 1918!

ÉDITH CRESSON
1st Woman President of France
1991 -1992.

Cresson's political career did not start with much success. She had worked hard for Mitterrand's first failed attempt for national office in 1965 and she lost her first race for Parliament in 1975. However, her fortunes changed in 1977 when she was elected mayor of Thure. Then in 1979, she was elected to the European Parliament in the E. U's first Parliamentary elections. She later went on to become mayor of Chatellerault.[ccxci]

In the 1980s she served President Mitterrand by her leadership in several departments: agriculture, tourism and foreign trade, industry and foreign trade, and European affairs. She became known for her outspokenness. [ccxcii]

Her term as Prime Minister was from 1991 – 1992. She set out ambitious plans to revitalize industry and help wage earners which failed when the economy slowed. President Mitterrand quickly replaced her. Her term was brief and plagued by financial and social upheaval.

She was appointed in 1995 to serve as European Commissioner for Science, Research, and Education. She was accused of hiring her dentist to advise the E.U on HIV/AIDS. She left office in 1999 and was charged in 2003. [ccxciii] She was found guilty of a reduced charge of favoritism but was not penalized.

KAZIMIRA PRUNSKIENE
1st Woman Prime Minister of Lithuania 1990 – 1991.

"A country only ruled by men cannot be considered a true democracy."

When Kazimira Prunskiene was a baby, her father, a beloved forest ranger and local musician, was murdered by the NKVD (the early KGB). Despite this, she eventually joined the Communist Party of Lithuania as it was the only political party at the time. She worked in academia and in 1986 she was appointed Deputy Director of the Agricultural Economics Research Institute. [ccxcvi] She was part of the leadership that helped create the independence movement in Lithuania. When Lithuania became the first Soviet S.S.R to declare its independence, Prunskiene was elected as its first Prime Minister. Her term lasted less than one year. The Soviet Union embargoed Lithuania to keep other Republics from breaking free. In her role, she travelled the world to garner respect and support for the fledgling nation.[ccxcvii]

Bergmann-Pohl taking charge and creating a democracy.

SABINE BERGMANN-POHL
The Only Woman Prime Minister of East Germany 1990.

"A quarter of a century after the fall of the iron curtain, borders within the E.U, have lost much of their significance."[ccxcviii]

A medical doctor and lung specialist by profession, Bergmann-Pohl was elected to the People's Chamber in the only free elections ever held in East Germany. She was elected President and served for six months in 1990 in a crucial time when this new East German Parliament voted to petition West Germany for reunification. She oversaw the application and peaceful transition during the re-unification process of the two Germanys which had been separated after World War Two. She served the unified Cabinet under Chancellor Kohl and in the Bundestag until 2002.

GRO HARLEM BRUNDTLAND
1st Woman Prime Minister of Norway
1981, 1986–1989, 1990–1996.

"I see the world health organization's role as being the moral voice and the technological leader in improving the health of the people of the world."

From a young age Brundtland had been interested in politics, medicine and the environment. After following in her father's

---

75 Wikipedia.

footsteps to become a doctor, she entered the Norwegian Ministry of Health. For a decade, she worked in the children's Department of the National Hospital and focused on children's medical issues. Over time, she became the Director of Health Services for the Children of Oslo, Norway's capital. [ccxcix]

Gro's domestic and international political Career spanned more than 45 years.

[76] In 1974, she was appointed Minister of the Environment of Norway. In this position her profile received national attention and she was appointed Prime Minister in 1981 when only 41 years old. She was the first female and youngest person in Norway's history to achieve this. Over the next 20 years, she became a fixture as part of the Norwegian political landscape, serving three terms as Prime Minister. [ccc] She always had close to 50% women in all of her Cabinets and worked hard to provide women equal access to workplace and educational opportunities. In the 1980s, she led the World Commission of Environment and Development, named after her - the Brundtland Commission. In 1983 she chaired the U.N World Commission on Environment and Development, which directly led to the Janeiro Earth Summit which is considered a milestone in environmental affairs. [ccci] After serving her last term as Prime Minister, she was appointed Director of the World Health Organization.

---

[76] Wikimedia Commons, both.

VIGDIS FINNBOGADOTTIR

1st Woman President of Iceland
1980 – 1996.

"I often speak at conferences on gender and notice that there are no men in the audience. I must underline the importance of education. Gender equality must be brought into each of us at an early age, through formal and informal education at home, at school and in society in general." [xxviii]

Born to a nurse and a civil engineer, Finnbogadottir attended the Sorbonne in France and soon joined an experimental theater group. She began her career as a Professor at the University of Iceland. She then became the Director of the Reykjavik Theater Company throughout the 1970s. During that time, she combined her teaching background and her new position by starring on a TV show highlighting culture in Iceland. [ccciii] Because of her popularity, she was drafted in 1980 as a candidate for President. It is a largely ceremonial

Vigdis at home in front of an adoring crowd [ccciv]

position. She won a plurality victory in a four-way field and was re-elected three times. She continued in humanitarian work and she established the Council of Women Leaders at Harvard University and served in the United Nations.

cccv

MARIA PINTASILGO
1st Woman Prime Minister of Portugal, 1979.

As a youth, Maria Pintasilgo joined a militaristic youth movement founded by the dictator Salazar. In school, she studied Chemical Engineering and worked for a large cement company, eventually as the Chief Engineer. [cccvi] In the early 1960s she joined a Catholic women's movement and worked to establish it in Portugal.

"I believe deeply that women can change society. Now that we are equal, let us dare to be different!"

77

She worked throughout the late 1960s and early 1970s in Portugal and internationally to promote women's issues and increase women's involvement in politics. By 1974 she was appointed Minister of Social Affairs, and in 1975 she became Ambassador to UNESCO. [cccvii]

Because she was well respected and well known, when there was a vacancy for Prime Minister, the President appointed her as Interim Prime Minister until an election could be held. During her three months in office she worked to make social security universal. She ran for President, in her own right, in 1986, but came in a distant third place. She was elected, however, to the European Parliament representing the Socialist Party. [cccviii]

---

[77] Wikimedia Commons.

MILKA PLANINC
1st Woman Prime Minister of Yugoslavia 1982 – 1986
Prime Minister of Croatia S.R, 1971 – 1982.

"My youth was spent at a time that assured me a life with a lot of substance. Those were dangerous times. I vividly recall very hard, very dramatic moments that left deep scars. Not only for me but for Yugoslavs as a people. What left the deepest imprint was the feeling of what people, as a group and as individuals, can do when they experience a unity of stance and of courage. 'Those were circumstances in which people can exceed themselves."[cccix]

In 1941 Nazi Germany invaded Yugoslavia. It took less than one month for the Yugoslavia to surrender, but Partisans attacked and fought the Nazis throughout the occupation. In 1944, a young 19-year-old Milka Planinc joined the Partisan rebels and the Communist Party. [cccx] She became the Commissar for the Dalmatian Partisan Brigade (Dalmatia is a local Province) in charge of Party loyalty. She was rumored to have been present at the Kocevje Pits massacre of fleeing Nazi sympathizers and their families where more than 10,000 perished. [cccxi cccxii cccxiii]

After World War Two, Yugoslavia was led for nearly forty years by Marshal Josip Tito, a World War Two Partisan hero and leader. Planinc held several posts within the local Communist Party after the war and was elevated to the Croatian Central Committee in 1959. [cccxiv] In 1966, she was elected to the Croatian Presidium. Within a year, she became President of the Assembly of Croatia until 1971. In 1971 a wave of gatherings and protests for a more liberal Croatia swept the nation. It was encouraged, in part, by the President of the Croatian Socialist Republic (S.R) Savka Kucar. To bring to an end the

'Croatian Spring,' Tito replaced Kucar at the helm with Planinc who arrested the leaders of the liberal and national awakening. When Tito died in 1980, a rotating power sharing agreement among the top S.R leaders of Yugoslavia was agreed upon with Planinc being elevated to Prime Minister in 1982, for four years. At the time, she was considered the first female Head of State of a Communist Nation. [cccxv cccxvi]

The achievements of her term included:

➢ Yugoslavia began paying its international debts.
➢ Austerity measures stabilized Yugoslavia's economy. [cccxvii]

MARGARET THATCHER
1st Woman Prime Minister in Europe and Great Britain
1979 – 1990.

"Defeat? I do not recognize the meaning of the word."

---

[78] Wikimedia Commons.

"If you just set out to be liked, you would be prepared to compromise on anything, and you would achieve nothing."[xxxviii]

Thatcher had a love for Conservative politics from an early age. She studied Chemistry at Oxford and became a Chemist, but her first love remained politics, and conservative politics at that. In 1950, a 26-year-old Thatcher ran for public office for the first time. Her first attempts were unsuccessful as she ran in a largely liberal area in an age when women rarely ran for office. But her strength and impressive speaking abilities made her known in both Conservative and Liberal circles.[79]

Golda Meir and Margaret Thatcher debate.

In the early 1960s, she held the Parliamentary Deputy Secretary and Shadow Minister positions while the Conservatives were out of power. When the Conservatives came back into power in 1970,

---

[79] Creative Commons.

Thatcher was appointed Minister for Education and Science. She earned the nickname "Thatcher, milk snatcher," after she ended free milk at public schools. She found that Prime Minister Heath, of her own party, wasn't receptive to her ideas. When the Conservatives fell out of power in 1974, she ran against Heath and won. A poor economy returned the Conservatives to power in 1979 and Margaret Thatcher was sworn in as the first female Prime Minister in British history. [cccxix] She gained a worldwide reputation as being a tough anti-communist. When the Argentinian Junta invaded the Falkland Islands, a group of barren islands the British owned off the Argentine coast, Thatcher sent the British fleet thousands of miles to defeat the Argentine fleet and retake the islands. Her main issues and successes of her three successive terms in office were, she:

➢ Won the Falkland Islands War against the Military Junta of Argentina.
➢ She cut social welfare programs.
➢ Privatized social housing and public transportation.
➢ Attempted to reduce the power of Unions in Britain.
➢ Was virulently anti-communist.

For a generation of European women, Thatcher was the face of women in politics.[cccxx] Many women leaders have subsequently been called "Iron Lady," but Margaret Thatcher was the original.

---

[80] Creative Commons.

SAVKA DABCEVIC KUCAR
1st Woman Prime Minister of Croatia S.R
(Not an Independent Nation)
1967 – 1969.

Savka Kucar was a young Partisan fighter during World War Two and became an important Croatian leader during the late 1960s – early 1970s. She worked her way up through the Yugoslavian Communist Party apparatus and became the first woman in Croatia, and one of the first women in the Communist world, to become Prime Minister. During her term, she famously took part in the "Croatian Spring," encouraging cultural and political reform. This effort was suppressed by the Yugoslavian government in part because

---

81 Photo Source: pjrc.library.utoronto.ca

of its nationalistic tendencies. She was forced to step down and resign from the party in 1971, because of this attempt at liberal reforms. [cccxxi] [cccxxii] [cccxxiii] She was replaced by Milka Planinc.

She remained popular in Croatia and when democracy came to her nation in 1992, she created a moderate party and ran unsuccessfully for President. [cccxxiv]

82

JACINDA ARDEN
Prime Minister of New Zealand 2017 -2023.[83]

We begin our final chapter of The Women's 100 with arguably the most successful national leader of recent modern times, Jacinda Arden. As a youth, she was elected to head the International Union of Socialist Youth. She became a researcher for Helen Clark's Office when she was Prime Minister and saw first-hand the inner workings of the Prime Minister. In 2008 she was elected to Parliament and rose in the ranks until, after a series of resignations at the highest level of party leadership, she was elected in 2017 to lead the Labour Party. After a brief stint as the Leader of the Opposition. As a result of the

---

elections, the Labour Party joined with the Green party and New Zealand First Party to form a minority government of which she was the Prime Minister. She was 37 years old and the youngest serving female head of state.

Often times a minority government in a Parliamentary system is the kiss of death for a young aspiring politician because it is so very difficult to gain a majority for legislative initiatives. By the end of her first term, so popular and successful was her administration that her party won an outright majority of over 50% and could govern alone if it chose, by the end of her second term, they was a staggering 60% majority. Shortly after her election, she gave birth in 2017, only the second woman in history after Benazir Bhutto, to do so as an elected head of state.

One of her actions was to respond to a mass shooting, one of the first in New Zealand, with gun control laws, which proved to be popular. When Covid broke out, she decisively closed New Zealand to foreign travel unless the traveler was quarantined for 14 days. As a result, the number of deaths from Covid was 3,347 instead of the projected 85,000. The public support and gratitude was felt at the voting polls. She moved to pass a bold legislative agenda and change the social support structure of New Zealand within a few years. During this time, she increased parental leave to 26 weeks, made school lunches free to help children from impoverished families, increased the minimum wage several times, increased teacher's pay, made passed reducing legislation and went out of her way to show respect for the native Maori customs.[84]

Preparing for a run for a third term, she was exhausted. She had done so much to keep her country safe and on the right path, but it took its toll. She wanted to now spend time with her family, so she did the unthinkable, she resigned at the height of her power and popularity. Ahern was arguably the best performing head of state at the time.

---

[84] https://en.wikipedia.org/wiki/Jacinda_Ardern

JULIA GILLARD
1st Woman Prime Minister of Australia
2010 – 2013.

"I will not be lectured about sexism and misogyny by this man. I will not. And the Government will not be lectured about sexism and misogyny by this man. Not now, not ever."[cccxxv]

Julia Gillard was born in Wales, Great Britain but her parents moved to Australia due to her childhood bronchitis. In College, Gillard became the second women to ever lead the Australian Union of Students and she served as a local President of the Labor Party in the late 1980s. [cccxxvi]

---

[85] Photo Credit: Googleplus.com

She studied law and became a partner at the age of 29. In her first forays into politics, she lost her first election attempts for Parliament. When she became Chief of Staff to the head of the Labor Party, she called for and received a 35% quota of women candidates for 'winnable parliament seats.' She is also credited with the founding of EMILY'S List, the fundraising giant for women candidates. She was elected to Parliament in 1998 and Chaired several important committees. [cccxxvii]

In the 2000s, Gillard served in the 'shadow government' (opposition cabinet) as Shadow Minister for Population and Immigration, for Reconciliation and Indigenous Affairs and finally for Shadow

Minister for Health. [cccxxviii] When Labor finally won in 2007, she was elevated to the position of Deputy Prime Minister for Australia. She was responsible for assuming the Presidential duties while President Ruud travelled abroad. During those times, she became known as one of Australia's most capable debaters and most competent administrators. [cccxxix] As President Ruud's popularity declined, Gillard challenged him for the leadership of the Labor Party. He withdrew and she was elected Prime Minister. [cccxxx] [86]

She was the first female elected Prime Minister and the first Australian Prime Minister not to have been married. [cccxxxi] Her focus at Prime Minister was on rejuvenating the economy that was damaged from the worldwide recession, add to add health services throughout Australia and passed a Clean Energy Bill in response to environmental groups and global warming. [cccxxxii]

---

[86] Wikipedia Commons.

HELEN CLARK
Prime Minister of New Zealand
1999 – 2008.

"No country will reach its full potential unless its female citizens enjoy full equality."

Helen Clark was a University Professor of Political Science at the University of Auckland in the 1970s. She was elected to the New Zealand Parliament in 1981 and held that seat for the next 28 years. During the 1980s, she served as Minister of Housing, Minister of Health, and Deputy Prime Minister. When her party was voted out of office she served as the Deputy Leader of the Opposition for four years and assumed leadership of her party in 1993. Finally, in 1999, her Labor Party was given a mandate in the elections and she became New Zealand's second female Prime Minister. [cccxxxiii]

During her time at the helm of New Zealand, the country experienced tremendous economic growth and surpluses. She served for three successive terms and by most accounts her terms were successful. During her term, New Zealand had:

➢ Become a leader in the world for sustainable, climate friendly growth.
➢ A stronger economy.
➢ Larger surpluses.
➢ Large investments into
➢ Low levels of unemployment.
➢ Large investments in education, health and elder care.
➢ Interest free student loans.
➢ Settled historical grievances with New Zealand's indigenous population.
➢ 14 weeks of paid parental leave. [cccxxxiv]
➢ Supported the Afghanistan War with troops and the Iraq War with materials, medical and engineering help. [cccxxxv cccxxxvi]

After retiring from New Zealand politics, she became and remains the Administrator of the United Nations Development Program. She is, of course, the first woman to hold that position.

Photo Source: iod.org.nz

[88]JENNIFER MARY SHIPLEY
1st Woman Prime Minister of New Zealand
1997 – 1999.

Jennifer Shipley began her career as a primary school teacher and member of several school organizations. She was a Member of Parliament from 1987 – 2002 and served as Minister of Social Welfare and Minister of Health through most of the 1990s. There was criticism of her leadership because of the cutbacks and

---

[88] Wikimedia Commons.

restructuring she led. In 1997, she led a successful political coup against her party's leader in his absence. However, two years later, she was defeated by Helen Clark, the second woman to run for Prime Minister in the 1999 election. She continued to lead the party after her defeat. In 2000, she had a stroke and retired from New Zealand politics in 2002. ^{cccxxxvii cccxxxviii}

ABOUT THE AUTHOR

Richard O'Brien was born in NYC and raised in Toronto, Canada and Sarasota, Florida. He is a product of Culver Academies, American University and Georgetown University. As a teacher, he instructed classes in *International Human Rights, Conflict in the Modern World* and *World Ideologies* at the University of South Florida and *World History, Women's Issues, American History, Geography and U.S Government* at the Duke Ellington School of the Arts in DC. A writer and human rights activist, he founded The Center for the Prevention of Genocide (CPG) from 2000 – 2004. The CPG actively worked to stop, intervene and prevent genocide, massacres, human rights violations and starvation in hotspots around the world. His human rights work has been featured in Business Insider and on the cover of Creative Loafing and he has been published in the Washington post and the New York Times, interviewed on National TV and NPR and has given testimony in Congressional Sub-Committee and at the United Nations. Subsequently, he has authored *Women Presidents and Prime Ministers*, 2017 and 201 editions and has a TED X lecture on the same subject. He has authored *Break Glass* featured on the next page about harrowing stories of genocide prevention and a road map to end genocide. Richard calls the DMV area and Florida his home, and is the proud father of twins, Annalise and John A.C. O'Brien.

JENOCO PUBLISHING www.jenoco.org
Jenoco Publishing is a forum used to publish human rights works, women's studies and the twenty or so unpublished manuscripts in the O'Brien family.

Break Glass: In Case of Genocide Break Glass – How We End Genocide. Author: Richard O'Brien. Experience the harrowing stories of 100 years of heroes who helped people escape genocide. Then, witness a group of student who recently raced against time and odds to prevent genocide in the modern age. "Stunning." "Way ahead of the bunch of us who have been writing and talking about intervention." "Riveting." "Wow, dark and powerful." $19.99. 258 pages. Abridged. Non-Fiction. www.jenoco.org . Bulk discount for 10 or more 55% $9.00 + S+H.

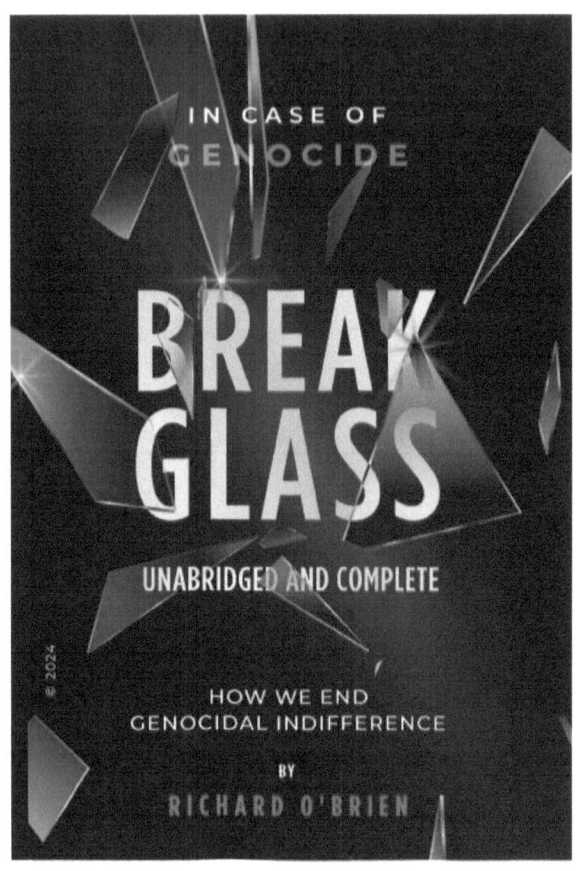

Break Glass Unabridged and Complete Richard O'Brien author. Material are from the CPG archives. includes all of Break Glass Abridged and features an additional 200 page book. The second book is a 'how-to manual' to create a human rights early warning system. Learn if you should, how to launch and how to successfully grow a human rights NGO that saves lives. Down to the granular details of how to write a press release, a country report, a micro report, how to advocate on the phone, in person and a myriad of other practical documents, lessons and steps if beginning a human rights NGO is your goal. $34.99. Non-Fiction. 432 pages. www.jenoco.org Bulk discount for 10 or more 55% $15.75 + S+H.

THE WOMEN'S 100: 100 Women Leaders of Nations and Peoples. Richard O'Brien author. Meet the more than 100 women who have served as leader of their respective nations and peoples around the world and learn the stories of their adventures, struggles and accomplishments. $19.99. Non-Fiction. Biography. www.jenoco.org . Bulk discount for 10 or more 55% $9.00 + S+H.

It's Like This. Jack O'Brien author.

Ecclesiastic muralist and President of the Canadian's Writer's Guild John (Jack) O'Brien loved his soulmate, knew the horrors of war and practiced his art passionately. He climbed up to church ceilings to paint them. He took his artist's pallet and wrote poetry that puts you on the battlefield, the bedroom and in his mind. Discover one of the powerhouse artistic talents of NYC during the 1950s and 1960s. $15.99 Poetry. Vivid imagery and profanity. www.jenoco.org . Bulk discount for 10 or more 55% $7.20 + S+H.

Touretters. Author/Editor Chris Mason and contributing authors have created a collection of rare and raw autobiographical stories written by individuals who are living with TS and their family members. This book helps demystify the condition and will touch your heart.

"This is a wonder-book." $19.99 Vivid imagery and language. Non-Fiction. Biography. www.jenoco.org . Bulk discount for 10 or more 55% $9.00 + S+H.

A Long Road Home. Dennis Maley author.
After losing her mother to cancer, 22-year old aspiring singer Jenny Harris couldn't be more alone. Enter T.K. Connolly, a debauched recluse of a writer who is revealed as her biological father and so begins a journey of self-discovery set in Savannah and New Orleans.

Fiction. $19.99. www.jenoco.org . Bulk discount for 10 or more 55% $9.00 + S+H.

TheFEEL. Matthew Mejia author. TheFEEL was Mejia's inaugural book of poetry and immediately caught fire. It is raw, powerful and vulnerable. Featured in Southern California College literature classes, Mejia is an emerging generational voice and talent. . "It brought back emotions I thought I left behind years ago." "I love, love this book! I finished the book in 2 hours!" "Matthew Mejia's scripture is real." "The most outstanding, bizarre, and relatable book I've read in ages." $15.99. Poetry. www.jenoco.org . Bulk discount for 10 or more 55% $7.20 + S+H.

[i] [i] Creative Commons

[ii] [ii] Wikipedia.

[iii] [iii] Creative Commons

[iv] Creative Commons.

[v] [v] Creative Commons.

[vi] [vi] Wikimedia Commons

[vii] Wikimedia Commons

[viii] [viii] Photo: Wikimedia Commons.

[ix] https://www.thenation.com/article/hillary-clintons-popular-vote-victory-is-unprecedented-and-still-growing/

[x] https://www.thenation.com/article/hillary-clintons-popular-vote-victory-is-unprecedented-and-still-growing/

Lynette Allston

[xi] https://en.wikipedia.org/wiki/Aleqa_Hammond

[xii] http://www.bbc.com/news/world-europe-18249813 **Aleqa Hammond**

[xiii] http://www.thelocal.dk/20141001/greenland-government-in-tatters-over-expenses-scandal

Kim Campbell

[xiv] [xiv] Britannica Kids

[xv] https://en.wikipedia.org/wiki/Kim_Campbell

[xvi] **Ibid.**

[xvii] http://www.kimcampbell.com/

Wilma Mankiller

[xviii] Wikimedia Commons.

[xix] Photo: Wikimedia Commons.

[xx] https://en.wikipedia.org/wiki/Portia_Simpson-Miller

[xxi] http://jis.gov.jm/profiles/portia-simpson-miller/

Laura Chinchilla [xxii] http://news.co.cr/wp-content/uploads/2012/04/President-Laura-Chinchilla1-300x277.jpg

[xxiii] http://www.rateaquote.com/cat/the+world+that/

[xxiv] http://politics.georgetown.edu/laura-chinchilla/

[xxv] **Ibid.**

Violeta Barrios de Chamorro

[xxvi] **Smartgirlsgroup.com**

[xxvii] https://www.britannica.com/biography/Laura-Chinchilla

[xxviii] Photo Source: Wikimedia Commons.

[xxix] https://www.youtube.com/watch?v=MoY_S8QaQag

Michele Pierre-Louis

[xxx] https://www.opensocietyfoundations.org/people/michele-pierre-louis

[xxxi] https://www.opensocietyfoundations.org/people/michele-pierre-louis

Portia Simpson-Miller

[xxxii] http://www.nytimes.com/1999/05/04/world/woman-in-the-news-mireya-elisa-moscoso-earnest-icon-for-panama.html

[xxxiii] Photo Credit: La Nacion

[xxxiv] https://www.britannica.com/biography/Violeta-Barrios-de-Chamorro

[xxxv] http://www.famousfix.com/topic/violeta-chamorro

[xxxvi] https://www.britannica.com/biography/Violeta-Barrios-de-Chamorro

[xxxvii] Photo Credit: San Diego Union Tribune

Dame Eugenia Charles [xxxviii] http://www.sandiegouniontribune.com/sdut-peacemaker-knows-ins-and-outs-power-2011oct20-htmlstory.html xxxix https://en.wikipedia.org/wiki/Claudette_Werleigh

xl Skard, Torild (2014) "Claudette Werleigh" in *Women of power - half a century of female presidents and prime ministers worldwide*, P. 64-65. Bristol: Policy Press

xli http://www.famousfix.com/topic/claudette-werleigh

xlii Bijoyeta Das (2011) *Building bridges, building peace, the life and work of Claudette Werleigh of Haiti*, University of San Diego: 2011 Women Peace Makers Programme
Ertha Pascal-Trouillot
xliii SUNY Manhattan EOC
Violeta de Chamorro xliv www.theguardian.com/news/2005/sep/08/guardianobituaries.pollypattullo

xlvi dccaribbeanbusinessdirectory.files.wordpress.com

xlvii Ibid.
xlviii https://en.wikipedia.org/wiki/Eugenia_Charles
xlix Photo: Creative Commons.
l http://www.biography.com/people/michelle-bachelet-37782
li http://michellebachelet.cl/pdf/biography.pdf

lii http://www.nytimes.com/2013/12/16/world/americas/bachelet-wins-chilean-presidency-in-landslide.html?rref=collection%2Ftimestopic%2FBachelet%2C%20Michelle&action=click&contentCollection=timestopics&region=stream&module=stream_unit&version=latest&contentPlacement=10&pgtype=collection

liii Photo: Creative Commons.
liv http://www.cnbc.com/2017/04/12/ousted-brazilian-president-dilma-rousseff-i-was-the-victim-of-a-coup.html
lv http://assets.bwbx.io/images/users/iqjWHBFdfxIU/imgW3ee72RmE/v2/-1x-1.jpg

Dilma Rousseff lvi http://www.bbc.com/news/world-latin-america-36028247

lvii http://www.nytimes.com/2012/08/05/world/americas/president-rousseffs-decades-old-torture-detailed.html?pagewanted=all
lviii Photo: Creative Commons.
Cristina Fernandez de Kirchner lix
https://en.wikipedia.org/wiki/Cristina_Fern%C3%A1ndez_de_Kirchner#Early_life_and_education
lx https://www.britannica.com/biography/Cristina-Fernandez-de-Kirchner
lxi Mtholyoak.edu
lxii http://remezcla.com
lxiii http://www.telesurtv.net/english/news/5-Great-Quotes-from-Argentinas-Cristina-Fernandez-20151025-0011.html
lxiv https://en.wikipedia.org/wiki/Cristina_Fern%C3%A1ndez_de_Kirchner
lxv Wikimedia Commons.
lxvi http://www.doonething.org/heroes/pages-j/jagan-quotes.htm
lxvii http://www.biography.com/people/janet-jagan-279082#peoples-progressive-party
lxviii Ibid.

[lxix] http://www.biography.com/people/janet-jagan-279082

Lidia Tejada [lxx] http://www.independent.co.uk/news/obituaries/lidia-gueiler-tejada-politician-who-became-only-the-wests-second-female-president-2282573.html
[lxxi] Incicliopedia, libre
[lxxii] https://en.wikipedia.org/wiki/Lidia_Gueiler_Tejada
[lxxiii] Ibid.
[lxxiv] Image: Wikipedia
[lxxv] Wikimedia Commons
[lxxvi]Wikipedia
Ellen Sirleaf
[lxxvii] Robinson, Jack. "Mrs. Sirleaf on 'Stimulating the Economy'". *Liberian Age*, 29 June 1973, pages 1–2.
[lxxviii] https://en.wikipedia.org/wiki/Ellen_Johnson_Sirleaf
[lxxix] *Kasuka, Bridgette (2016-10-11). Prominent African Leaders since Independence. New Africa Press. ISBN 9789987160266.*
[lxxx] https://en.wikipedia.org/wiki/Ellen_Johnson_Sirleaf
Ameenah Gurib-Fakim
[lxxxi] Photo: Nic Bothma.
[lxxxii] **studentsforliberty.org**
[lxxxiii]
https://www.ted.com/talks/ameenah_gurib_fakim_humble_plants_that_hide_surprising_secrets
[lxxxiv] **Informante**
[lxxxv]https://www.newera.com.na/2015/03/12/profile-saara-kuugongelwa-amadhila/
[lxxxvi] http://allafrica.com/stories/201503120490.html
[lxxxvii] https://www.wilsoncenter.org/event/conversation-the-right-honourable-saara-kuugongelwa-amadhila-prime-minister-the-republic
[lxxxviii] Informante
[lxxxix] Ibid.
Sheikh Hasina
[xc] https://en.wikipedia.org/wiki/Catherine_Samba-Panza
[xci]Wikimedia Commons

Catherine Samba-Panza
[xciv] http://dayagainsthomophobia.org/feminist-and-human-rights-activist-aminata-toure-new-senegal-prime-minister/
[xcv] https://www.theguardian.com/world/2013/sep/05/senegal-prime-minister-aminata-toure
[xcvi] Ibid.
[xcvii] https://en.wikipedia.org/wiki/Aminata_Tour%C3%A9
[xcviii] http://www.bbc.com/news/world-africa-28167389
Adiatu Nandigna
[xcix] Wikimedia Commons
[c] January 1, 2004, issue of *The Banker*
Luisa Diogo
[ci] http://www.notablebiographies.com/news/Ca-Ge/Diogo-Luisa.html
[cii] Ibid.
Joyce Banda
[cii] http://www.joycebandafoundation.com/about-us.html
[cii] Ibid.
Aminata Toure
[ciii] Wikimedia Commons.

civ Wikipedia Commons.

cv https://en.wikipedia.org/wiki/Sheikh_Hasina

cvi http://www.thefamouspeople.com/profiles/sheikh-hasina-5680.php

cvii http://www.somewhereinblog.net/blog/mrsumon007/29521188

cviii https://en.wikipedia.org/wiki/Sheikh_Hasina#The_1991.E2.80.931996_period

cix http://www.thefamouspeople.com/profiles/sheikh-hasina-5680.php

cx https://en.wikipedia.org/wiki/Sheikh_Hasina

Aung San Suu Kyi

cxi Wikimedia Commons.

cxii Photo Credit: GuaAnakMelaka

cxiii http://www.biography.com/people/aung-san-suu-kyi-9192617#awards-and-recognition

Tsai lng-wen

cxiv http://www.biography.com/people/aung-san-suu-kyi-9192617

cxv **Ibid.**

cxvi http://www.bbc.com/news/world-asia-pacific-11685977

cxvii Wikipedia Commons.

cxviii http://thehimalayantimes.com/kathmandu/who-is-bidhya-devi-bhandari/

cxix http://www.independent.co.uk/news/world/asia/bidhya-devi-bhandari-communist-activist-elected-nepal-s-first-female-president-a6712561.html

cxx https://www.theguardian.com/world/2015/oct/28/nepalese-parliament-first-female-president-bidhya-devi-bhandari

Angela Merkel

cxxi Wikipedia.

cxxii http://www.straitstimes.com/asia/east-asia/taiwans-first-woman-president-10-things-you-should-know-about-tsai-ing-wen

cxxiii **Ibid.**

cxxiv *"Taiwan gets first female President as DPP sweeps election". Channel NewsAsia. Retrieved 2016-01-16.*

cxxv https://en.wikipedia.org/wiki/Tsai_Ing-wen#cite_ref-:0_34-0

Bidhya Bhandari

cxxvi China Wiki

cxxvii http://www.bbc.com/news/world-asia-20787271

cxxviii http://www.korea.net/Government/Administration/President-Park-Geun-hye

cxxix http://www.thefamouspeople.com/profiles/park-geun-hye-6895.php#S78tkX8vucvyZsp7.99

cxxx http://www.cnn.com/2014/03/04/world/asia/south-koreas-first-female-president/

cxxxi http://www.bbc.com/news/world-asia-20787271

cxxxii https://www.britannica.com/biography/Park-Geun-Hye

cxxxiii http://qz.com/827571/south-koreas-president-park-geun-hye-said-tragedy-and-loneliness-drove-her-to-rely-on-choi-soon-sil-a-shadowy-female-confidante/

cxxxiv http://www.thefamouspeople.com/profiles/park-geun-hye-6895.php

cxxxv http://www.forbes.com/sites/ralphjennings/2016/11/02/south-korean-president-park-geun-hye-and-her-agenda-are-finished/#1aaf355053b3

Sheikh Hasina

http://www.thefamouspeople.com/profiles/sheikh-hasina-5680.php#VzF0pHbHhvlVGkfQ.99

cxxxvi https://en.wikipedia.org/wiki/Thaksin_Shinawatra

cxxxvii http://www.bbc.com/news/world-asia-pacific-13723451

cxxxviii http://www.bbc.com/news/world-asia-pacific-13723451

cxxxix http://www.bbc.com/news/world-asia-36422838

cxl Photo: Wikipedia

223

cxli http://izquotes.com/quote/257410

Roza Otunabayeva

cxlii http://carnegieendowment.org/2011/12/29/background-on-roza-otunbayeva-pub-46368

cxliii Ibid.

cxliv https://www.britannica.com/biography/Roza-Otunbayeva
cxlv Photo: Simple English Wikipedia.
cxlvi http://www.inspiringquotes.us/quotes/AgLD_RTPH8672
Gloria Arroyo cxlvii https://en.wikipedia.org/wiki/Gloria_Macapagal_Arroyo
cxlviii Photo: Simple English Wikipedia
cxlix https://www.britannica.com/biography/Khaleda-Zia
cl http://indianexpress.com/article/world/world-news/arrest-warrant-against-khaleda-zia-for-celebrating-birthday-on-aug-15-4380402/
cli https://www.britannica.com/biography/Khaleda-Zia
Chandrika Kumaratunga
clii http://www.quotes.net/authors/Chandrika%20Kumaratunga
cliii https://en.wikipedia.org/wiki/Chandrika_Kumaratunga
cliv Ibid.
clv *"'Dictatorship' cries after parliament suspended"*. *ABC Radio Australia. 2012. Retrieved 18 August 2016.*
Han Myeong-sook
clvi https://en.wikipedia.org/wiki/List_of_Presidents_of_Indonesia
clvii *Megawati's Intervention Prevents Massacre in Sulawesi,* Center for the Prevention of Genocide, 2002.
clviii http://biography.yourdictionary.com/megawati-sukarnoputri
Chang Sang
clix https://en.wikipedia.org/wiki/Tansu_%C3%87iller
clx https://www.britannica.com/biography/Tansu-Ciller
Benazir Bhutto
clxi http://quotesgram.com/popular/benazir-bhutto-quotes/
clxii **"Bhutto's Last Words." You Tube Video:**
https://www.youtube.com/watch?v=XMvL1W_Jgz8&feature=related
clxiii https://www.britannica.com/biography/Benazir-Bhutto

clxiv https://www.ctforum.org/panelist/benazir-bhutto

clxv http://www.history.com/topics/womens-history/benazir-bhutto
clxvi Ibid.
clxvii http://www.history.com/topics/womens-history/benazir-bhutto
Corazon 'Cory' Aquino
clxviii https://www.pinterest.com/pin/452259987560646175/
clxix http://www.filipiknow.net/facts-about-cory-aquino/
clxx
http://www.brainyquote.com/quotes/authors/c/corazon_aquino.html?gclid=CjwKEAiAu6DBBRD
Dr6e_6698E0SJACvuxny4ZffmFG_3whoH2uoykksQab1kz6TWttE5V-pGaFMPhoChJfw_wcB
clxxi http://www.amazingwomeninhistory.com/corazon-aquino-revolutionary-president-philippines/
clxxii http://www.amazingwomeninhistory.com/corazon-aquino-revolutionary-president-philippines/
clxxiii Ibid.
clxxiv https://en.wikipedia.org/wiki/Corazon_Aquino

Golda Meir
clxxv http://www.jewishvirtuallibrary.org/jsource/biography/meir.html
clxxvi https://www.brainyquote.com/quotes/authors/g/golda_meir.html

clxxvii http://www.jewishvirtuallibrary.org/jsource/biography/meir.html
clxxviii **Ibid.**
clxxix https://www.pixcove.com/tag/golda-meir/
clxxx www.brainyquote.com
clxxxi http://www.myinterestingfacts.com/wp-content/uploads/2014/02/Golda-Meir-Old.jpg

clxxxii http://www.jewishvirtuallibrary.org/jsource/biography/meir.html

Soong Qingling clxxxiii https://www.tripadvisor.co.uk/LocationPhotoDirectLink-g294212-d456974-i112332299-Peking_Former_Residence_of_Soong_Ching_Ling_Song_Qingling_Guju-Beijing.html
clxxxiv https://en.wikipedia.org/wiki/Kuomintang
clxxxv
https://en.wikipedia.org/wiki/President_of_the_People%27s_Republic_of_China#List_of_presidents
clxxxvi https://en.wikipedia.org/wiki/Soong_Ching-ling
Sirimavo Bandaranaike
clxxxvii http://www.newworldencyclopedia.org/entry/S%C3%B2ng_Q%C3%ACngl%C3%ADng
Indira Gandhi
clxxxviii
https://www.google.com/search?q=indira+gandhi+free+images&biw=1366&bih=635&source=lnms&tbm=isch&sa=X&ved=0ahUKEwjG5KyAn5fQAhWp5oMKHUv0BIUQ_AUIBigB#imgrc=44NL5U4XUTi2SM%3A
clxxxix https://en.wikipedia.org/wiki/Indira_Gandhi
cxc http://www.history.com/topics/indira-gandhi
cxci http://www.history.com/topics/indira-gandhi
cxcii http://policydialogue.org/files/events/Fujita_green_rev_in_india.pdf
cxciii https://en.wikipedia.org/wiki/Rajiv_Gandhi
cxciv *In Case of Genocide – Break Glass,* O'Brien, 2015.
cxcv https://en.wikipedia.org/wiki/Indira_Gandhi
cxcvi https://en.wikipedia.org/wiki/Rajiv_Gandhi
cxcvii Skard, Torild "Sirimavo Bandaranaike" and "Chandrika Kumaratunga", 2014

cxcviii https://en.wikipedia.org/wiki/Sirimavo_Bandaranaike

cxcix **Ibid.**
cc http://www.thefamouspeople.com/profiles/sirimavo-bandaranaike-7187.php

cci https://en.wikipedia.org/wiki/Sirimavo_Bandaranaike

Yadgar Nasriddinova

ccii http://free-images.gatag.net/images/201107140600.jpg (cropped)
cciii http://www.brainyquote.com/quotes/authors/a/angela_merkel_3.html

cciv https://en.wikipedia.org/wiki/Angela_Merkel

ccv *"Merkel named as German chancellor".* BBC News. 10 October 2005.

225

ccvi https://www.theguardian.com/world/2015/jan/07/ten-reasons-angela-merkel-germany-chancellor-world-most-powerful-woman
ccvii https://en.wikipedia.org/wiki/Greek_government-debt_crisis
ccviii http://www.forbes.com/profile/angela-merkel/
Dalia Grybauskaite
ccix
http://www.slate.com/articles/news_and_politics/foreigners/2014/09/russia_and_ukraine_lithuanian_president_dalia_grybauskaite_says_vladimir.html

ccx
http://www.slate.com/articles/news_and_politics/foreigners/2014/09/russia_and_ukraine_lithuanian_president_dalia_grybauskaite_says_vladimir.html

ccxi **http://www.thefemaleleaders.xyz/2016_07_01_archive.html**

ccxii https://en.wikipedia.org/wiki/Dalia_Grybauskait%C4%97

ccxiii **Ibid.**

ccxiv http://www.politico.eu/article/the-baltic-iron-lady-putins-solitary-foe-dalia-grybauskaite/

ccxv
http://www.slate.com/articles/news_and_politics/foreigners/2014/09/russia_and_ukraine_lithuanian_president_dalia_grybauskaite_says_vladimir.html

ccxvi https://en.wikipedia.org/wiki/Erna_Solberg

ccxvii https://www.theguardian.com/technology/2016/oct/05/norway-prime-minister-caught-playing-pokemon-go-parliament-erna-solberg
ccxviii http://www.bbc.com/news/world-europe-34619037
ccxix **Ibid.**
ccxx https://en.wikipedia.org/wiki/Beata_Szyd%C5%82o#cite_note-5
Kolinda Grabarkitarovi
ccxxi http://www.vecernji.hr/hrvatska/ekskluzivno-u-vecernjem-listu-veliki-politicki-intervju-kolinde-grabar-kitarovic-948570/multimedia/p1
ccxxii http://www.euronews.com/2015/06/29/croatian-president-kolinda-grabar-kitarovic-from-peace-recession-to-feminism

ccxxiii http://www.thefamouspeople.com/profiles/kolinda-grabar-kitarovi-6858.php#iect6bJKw6UlZZUw.99
ccxxiv https://www.theguardian.com/commentisfree/2016/jul/07/theresa-may-britain-tory-candidate
ccxxv http://www.independent.co.uk/news/uk/politics/theresa-may-brexit-means-brexit-conservative-leadership-no-attempt-remain-inside-eu-leave-europe-a7130596.html
Kersti Kaljulaid
ccxxvi **Estonianworld.com**
ccxxvii Former European auditor Kersti Kaljulaid elected president of Estonia **Estonian World, 2 October 2016. Accessed on 3 October 2016.**
ccxxviii **Ibid.**
ccxxix http://www.scmp.com/news/world/europe/article/2027010/estonia-swears-biologist-turned-banker-kersti-kaljulaid-first
Beata Szydo

ccxxx **Atifete Jahjaga** https://news.dartmouth.edu/news/2016/06/former-kosovo-president-begins-montgomery-fellowship

Tarja Halonen

ccxxxi http://www.aljazeera.com/programmes/women-make-change/2015/10/road-kosovo-female-president-151021070704139.html

ccxxxii https://en.wikipedia.org/wiki/Laimdota_Straujuma

ccxxxiii **Ibid.**

ccxxxv http://www.ft.dk/Folketinget/findMedlem/SHETS.aspx

Helle Thorning-Schmidt

ccxxxvi *"Danish opposition wins vote, delivering first woman PM | Deccan Herald".* *Deccanherald.com. 16 September 2011.*

ccxxxvii https://en.wikipedia.org/wiki/Helle_Thorning-Schmidt

Vassiliki Thanou

ccxxxviii *SF leaves government, Vilhelmsen steps down". The Copenhagen Post. 30 January 2014. Retrieved 30 January 2014.*

ccxxxix Photo Source: Britannica.com

ccxl https://en.wikipedia.org/wiki/J%C3%B3hanna_Sigur%C3%B0ard%C3%B3ttir#cite_note-salon1-36

Joanna Sigurdardottir ccxli http://www.advocate.com/politics/politicians/2013/05/03/legacy-worlds-first-out-lesbian-prime-minister

Laimdota Straujuma

ccxlii http://www.azquotes.com/author/20391-Tarja_Halonen

ccxliii https://en.wikipedia.org/wiki/Tarja_Halonen

ccxliv **Ibid.**

ccxlv Photo Source: pjrc.library.utoronto.ca

Iveta Radicova ccxlvi *"Iveta Radičová". The Slovak Spectator*

ccxlvii **Ibid.**

ccxlviii http://www.famousfix.com/topic/iveta-radiova

ccxlix *Radičová sa rozlúčila, aby sa mohla vrátiť*

ccl https://en.wikipedia.org/wiki/Iveta_Radi%C4%8Dov%C3%A1

ccli http://2governmentquotes.blogspot.com/2016/06/top-10-famous-female-prime-ministers.html

Jadranka Kosor

cclii **Quotefancy.com**

ccliii *"One Heart at a Time". Harvard Kennedy School. Winter–Spring 1999.*

ccliv https://en.wikipedia.org/wiki/Mary_McAleese

cclv *"Mary McAleese an amazon in Ireland's political scene". Saturday Tribune. 9 April 2011.* http://2.bp.blogspot.com/-anfavB1TTU/UL4Go0NA3YI/AAAAAAAAF4I/qg8EqVkkFeU/s1600/FullC22289D2011-01-01.jpg.png

cclvii http://www.famousfix.com/topic/jadranka-kosor

cclviii https://en.wikipedia.org/wiki/Jadranka_Kosor

cclix https://sussle.org/t/Jadranka_Kosor

cclx **Ibid.**

Zinaida Greceanii
cclxi Greceanii.md

cclxii Wikipedia http://www.famousfix.com/topic/zinaida-greceanii

cclxiii Page on Greceanii at government website Archived
cclxiv "Moldova's Leader Nominates First Female Prime Minister"[permanent dead link], Associated Press (*The Moscow Times*), 24 March 2008.
cclxv Skard, Torild (2014) "Zinaida Greceanîi" in *Women of power - half a century of female presidents and prime ministers worldwide*, Bristol, Policy Press P. 359
cclxvi http://news.bbc.co.uk/2/hi/europe/8059039.stm;
http://news.bbc.co.uk/2/hi/europe/8071251.stm; www.ipu.org/parline-e/reports/2215_E.htm
cclxvii Photo Source: Twitter
cclxviii Nino Burjanadze Photo Credit: Russian Times
cclxix Women of power: Half a century of female presidents and prime minister, Torid Skard.

Radmila Sekerinska cclxxi M.independent.mk
cclxxi Photo Credit: Ionepine
cclxxii https://en.wikipedia.org/wiki/Social_Democratic_Union_of_Macedonia
cclxxiii https://en.wikipedia.org/wiki/Radmila_%C5%A0ekerinska
cclxxiv http://www.famousfix.com/topic/radmila-ekerinska
Ewa Kopacz
cclxxv The Apricity Forum
Natasha Micic
cclxxvi http://www.invest-in-serbia.com/tws/presidential_election_2002/2002_12_16_1.htm
cclxxvii http://www.sfgate.com/politics/article/She-s-young-beautiful-and-Serbia-s-new-leader-2686279.php
Reneta Indzhova
cclxxviii https://en.wikipedia.org/wiki/Nata%C5%A1a_Mi%C4%87i%C4%87
Mary Robinson cclxxix AZ Quotes
cclxxx http://www.mrfcj.org/about/board-of-trustees/mary-robinson-chair-of-the-board-of-trustees/
cclxxxi http://www.ohchr.org/EN/AboutUs/Pages/Robinson.aspx
cclxxxii http://articles.chicagotribune.com/1993-06-11/news/9306110023_1_ms-suchocka-hanna-suchocka-polish-parliament
cclxxxiii Photo Source: Nowa Historia
cclxxxiv https://en.wikipedia.org/wiki/Hanna_Suchocka
cclxxxv Ibid.
cclxxxvi Opfell (1993) "Hanna Suchocka" in *Women prime ministers and presidents*, Jefferson, NC: McFarland & Co, ISBN 978-0899507903, pp. 212-22; Skard, Torild (2014) "Hanna Suchocka" in *Women of power - Half a century of female presidents and prime ministers worldwide*, Bristol: Policy Press, ISBN 978-1-44731-578-0, pp. 344-5
cclxxxvii http://articles.chicagotribune.com/1993-06-11/news/9306110023_1_ms-suchocka-hanna-suchocka-polish-parliament
cclxxxviii Lewis, Jone Johnson (1992) *Hanna Suchocka government*, October, www.womenshistory.about.com and *Who's Who in Poland, Directory of members of parliament, state and local government and the presidential chancellery 1994-1995*, (1994) Warsaw, p.II-497
cclxxxix Siemienska, Renata (2003) "Women in the Polish Sejm" in R.E. Matland and K.A. Montgomery (eds) *Women's access to political power in post-communist Europe*, Oxford/New York, NY: Oxford University Press, pp. 217-44
Edith Cresson
ccxc mediamass

ccxci https://www.britannica.com/biography/Edith-Cresson

228

ccxcii Ibid.

ccxciii https://en.wikipedia.org/wiki/%C3%89dith_Cresson
Anneli Jaatteenmaki

ccxciii http://www.famousfix.com/topic/anneli-jaatteenmaki

ccxciv http://www.komentaras.lt/wp-content/uploads/2011/03/Kazimiera-Villon_680.jpg
ccxcv Women of Power: Half a Century of Female Presidents and Prime Ministers, Torrid Skard, P. 338, 2006 interview.
ccxcvi Opfell, Olga. Women Prime Ministers and Presidents. Jefferson, North Carolina: McFarland and Co., 1993.
Kazimira Prunskiene
ccxcvii http://jagahost.proboards.com/thread/19725/lithuania-election-farmers-party-triumph
ccxcviii https://www.bundestag.de/en/documents/textarchive/kw26_lammert_knesset_en/380096

Gro Brundtland ccxcix http://www.un.org/News/dh/hlpanel/brundtland-bio.htm

ccc Ibid.
ccci https://en.wikipedia.org/wiki/Gro_Harlem_Brundtland
Jadranka Kosor
cccii https://www.youtube.com/watch?v=JIVXp3TSS_w
ccciii https://www.britannica.com/biography/Vigdis-Finnbogadottir
Sabine Bergmann-Pohl
ccciv http://activistswithattitude.com/icelandic-women-take-a-day-off-and-then-another/
Maria Pintasilgo
cccv *Sisterhood is Global*, p. 575; photo http://bit.ly/x9pv4p
cccvi Associated Press, *International News*, Lisbon, Portugal, 19 July 1979
cccvii Associated Press, *International News*, Lisbon, Portugal, 19 July 1979
cccviii "Maria de Lourdes Pintasilgo", p. 32, *The Times (London)*, 15 July 2004
Milka Planinc
cccix http://www.nytimes.com/1985/05/19/world/yugoslav-preparing-for-us-trip-acknowledges-economic-decline.html
cccx *Opfell, Olga S. (1993). Women Prime Ministers and Presidents. Jefferson, North Carolina: McFarlane & Company*
cccxi "Kardelj's dispatches found", B92
cccxii https://en.wikipedia.org/wiki/Ko%C4%8Devski_Rog_massacre
cccxiii 24ur.com
cccxiv *Opfell, Olga S. (1993). Women Prime Ministers and Presidents. Jefferson, North Carolina: McFarlane & Company. P112*
cccxv https://en.wikipedia.org/wiki/Milka_Planinc#cite_note-Guardian-obituary-1
cccxvi Pjrc.library.utoronto.ca
cccxvii https://en.wikipedia.org/wiki/Milka_Planinc
Margaret Thatcher
cccxviii Superbcommunication.com
cccxix http://www.biography.com/people/margaret-thatcher-9504796#britains-first-female-premier
cccxx Nadezhda Grekova https://s-media-cache-ak0.pinimg.com/originals/5a/e1/5c/5ae15c7d306caf63d8c7102c419e6031.jpg
cccxxi https://en.wikipedia.org/wiki/Croatian_Spring
cccxxii https://en.wikipedia.org/wiki/Savka_Dab%C4%8Devi%C4%87-Ku%C4%8Dar

Nadezhda Grekova

[cccxxv] http://www.smh.com.au/federal-politics/political-news/transcript-of-julia-gillards-speech-20121009-27c36.html
[cccxxvi] *"The Hon Julia Gillard MP, Member for Lalor (Vic)"*. *Australian House of Representatives.*

[cccxxvii] https://en.wikipedia.org/wiki/Julia_Gillard

[cccxxviii] *Crean names new team"*. *ABC News. 18 February 2003. Archived from the original on 25 April 2006.*
[cccxxix] **Ibid.**
[cccxxx] Photo Source pm.gov.au
[cccxxxi] **Ibid**
[cccxxxii] *"Carbon tax gets green light in Senate: SMH 8 November 2011"*. *The Sydney Morning Herald. 8 November 2011.*

Helen Clark [cccxxxiii] https://en.wikipedia.org/wiki/Helen_Clark

[cccxxxiv] *"Historical Dictionary of Polynesia"*. *google.co.uk.*
[cccxxxv] http://www.undp.org/content/undp/en/home/operations/leadership/administrator/biography.html

[cccxxxvi] https://en.wikipedia.org/wiki/Helen_Clark

Jennifer Shipley [cccxxxvii] **Wikipedia**
[cccxxxviii] http://www.famousfix.com/topic/jenny-shipley

www.ingramcontent.com/pod-product-compliance
Lightning Source LLC
Chambersburg PA
CBHW020446130626
46549CB00001B/317